IDEAS FOR SCIENCE PROJECTS

ROBERT GARDNER

AN EXPERIMENTAL
SCIENCE SERIES BOOK

FRANKLIN WATTS
NEW YORK / LONDON
TORONTO / SYDNEY / 1986

Diagrams by Vantage Art

Photographs courtesy of:
the author: pp. 18, 96;
#210285, American Museum of Natural History: p. 20;
The Yerkes Observatory: p. 56;
Ward's Natural Science Establishment, Inc.: pp. 60, 136;
Carolina Biological Supply Company: p. 123.

Library of Congress Cataloging in Publication Data
Gardner, Robert.
Ideas for science projects.

(An Experimental science series book)
Bibliography: p.
Includes index.
Summary: Introduces the scientific method through
instructions for observations and experiments in biology,
physics, astronomy, botany, psychology, and chemistry.
1. Science—Experiments—Juvenile literature [1. Science
—Experiments   2. Experiments]
I. Title.   II. Series.
Q164.G37 1986   507'.8   87-9238
ISBN 0-531-10246-7

CONTENTS

IDEAS FOR SCIENCE PROJECTS

Other books by Robert Gardner

Backyard Science
Kitchen Chemistry
Magic Through Science
Save That Energy
Science Around the House
Space: Frontier of the Future
The Whale Watchers' Guide
The Young Athlete's Manual
This Is the Way It Works
Water: The Life Sustaining Resource

INTRODUCTION

Scientists solve problems by making careful observations, carrying out experiments, putting known information together in novel ways, or a combination of all of these. Doing a science project will help you understand how a scientist works. You will make observations, conduct experiments, try to draw conclusions or formulate hypotheses based on evidence, and report your findings.

In most of the projects in this book, you will find a number of questions that you can answer by doing experiments. For example, the question "Does a dehumidifier really reduce the moisture in a house?" can be answered by measuring the humidity before and after a dehumidifier is turned on.

While doing projects suggested in this book, you may discover new questions that you can answer through experiments of your own design. By all means carry out these experiments after consulting with an adult to be sure that they are safe. You are developing the kind of curiosity that characterizes a good scientist.

In his book *How to Do a Science Project*, David Webster writes, "Perhaps the hardest part of doing a science project is getting an idea to work on." It's reasonable to ask which brand of paper towel absorbs the most water. But it makes no sense to ask Bill Cosby's famous question "What's air for?" or Why is there gravity? because these questions simply have no answers.

The purpose of this book is to provide some ideas to work on. Some of the projects are simply questions designed to stimulate inquiry. Others contain fairly detailed instructions about how to proceed, but even these usually include a little food for thought that could lead to more individual inquiry. If you're new to the game of science, you might like to start with a project that is described quite thoroughly. After you've done some science, you may prefer to pursue more open-ended projects.

This book contains more projects than you could ever do, and there is a wide variety of topics. It might be good to do some projects from different chapters in an effort to find where your interests lie. Some people say, "I don't like biology," or "I don't like physics" without ever trying it. Once you get into a project, you may find it's a lot more interesting and challenging than you expected.

THE METHODS OF SCIENCE

You may have heard that science projects will teach you the *scientific method*. Despite what you've heard, no fixed method is followed in science. Each question must be pursued in a unique manner; however, some principles or components are common to all modes of scientific inquiry. They include reference to authority, use of the senses, trial and error, experimental controls, repetition, and experimental errors.

SAFETY FIRST

1. Maintain a serious attitude while conducting experiments. Do not fool around. It can be dangerous to you and to others.

2. Read instructions carefully before proceeding with an experiment if it is one described in this book. If you have questions, check with a knowledgeable adult before you begin the activity.

3. If you are designing an experiment of your own, check with a responsible and knowledgeable adult before you actually carry out the experiment. There might be a flaw in your design that could produce an accident.

4. Wear protective goggles over your eyes whenever you are doing chemical experiments or any other experiment that could lead to eye damage.

5. Do not touch chemicals with your bare hands unless instructed to do so. **Wash your hands after conducting experiments involving chemicals.**

6. Do not taste dry chemicals or solutions. Do not eat food while conducting experiments.

7. Do not inhale fumes released during a chemical reaction. Experiments involving any poisonous or irritating gases should be done in a fume hood.

8. Keep flammable materials away from heat sources.

9. Keep the area in which you are working clean and organized. Make sure that nothing, such as gas or electricity, is left on when not being used.

10. Have safety equipment such as fire extinguishers, fire blankets, safety showers, and first aid equipment available while you are experimenting. Know where this equipment is.

11. Clean up chemical spills immediately. If you spill anything on your skin or clothing, rinse it off immediately with plenty of water, then report what happened to a responsible adult.

12. Be careful about touching glass that has recently been heated; it looks the same as cool glass. Bathe any skin burns in cool water or apply ice.

A scientist generally begins research by consulting books and journals to see what others have found about the topic in question. In most of the ideas suggested in this book, it would be better to proceed on your own so that you develop a sense of exploring what is the unknown to you, even if the question has been answered by others. In a few cases, some reference to authority is suggested to get you started.

Scientists use their senses—sight, hearing, touch, smell, and taste—to observe data related to their questions. They have also invented microscopes, telescopes, chemical tests, and various measuring devices to extend their senses.

In many cases, where a variety of causes are suspected, a scientist will try first one thing and then another in a trial-and-error fashion, looking for the one that gives the desired effect.

Where possible, scientists have experimental controls; that is, they test the effect of a single variable. For example, suppose you think temperature affects the rate at which water evaporates. You would take two samples of water, exactly the same in every respect except that one sample is warm and the other cold. If the warm water evaporates faster, you have made your case. However, if the warm water had been in an environment where the wind was blowing, while the cold water sat in an enclosed box, you could not be sure whether increased evaporation was due to temperature or wind.

Repetition is vital to science. Experimental results must be repeatable. If your data does not agree with that of someone else who does the same experiment, scientists will not accept the conclusions you make because they are based on data that cannot be confirmed.

No matter how careful you are, every experiment contains errors. You can measure something with a ruler to no better than 0.1 millimeter (mm); the temperatures that you measure are no more accurate than the thermometers you use to measure them; the time periods you obtain depend on the watch or stopwatch you use. Observations depend on the number of times you see one thing as opposed to something else. You might see 1,000 robins flying south and decide that robins were migrating. Then on the next day you see 800 robins flying south and 200 flying north. Now all you can say is that 90 percent of the robins seem to be flying south.

Experimental errors are relative. To an astronomer, a difference of a light-year from one measurement to another may be insignificant, but to an atomic physicist a difference of 10^{-10} meters (m), in two measurements may destroy a theory.

THE NOTEBOOK

As you start a project, keep a notebook, preferably a spiral book that includes graph paper so that you can make graphs of your data or scaled drawings of experimental equipment or designs. Record what you do, data you collect, and tentative conclusions you make. Be as thorough as possible. You may think you'll remember an observation, but a week later you will have forgotten and you'll have to repeat the experiment. If it is based on something you saw in nature, that may not be possible.

THE PLAN

Begin your project by writing a statement of the problem you are pursuing. This is usually a question. Then write out a plan that you intend to follow in attacking the problem. Your plan might include equipment you'll need, drawings, and a time schedule. Recognize that your plan may be subject to change. All scientists expect problems. Things seldom work out as planned; if they did, science would be far less challenging than it is. There will be breakage, leaks, or seeds that fail to germinate; there will be mistakes, data that makes no sense, and a failure to control some unexpected variable. Don't be concerned if your project does not lead to a simple, neat conclusion. It's the process that's important, and you can prepare an interesting display for a science fair that reports your ongoing, unfinished research and the questions that remain unanswered based on the data you have collected.

THE PROJECT REPORT

If you plan to enter your project in a science fair, you should write a detailed report that includes:

- acknowledgment of those who helped you in any way.
- the problem you investigated and your motivation for pursuing it.
- a discussion of what you did and why.
- the results you obtained. Charts, drawings, graphs, and photographs will help to make your display more interesting and attractive. Graphs should be plotted with straight lines or smooth curves. Don't connect each point immediately. If you repeat the experiment several times (remember repeatability), the points you obtain will cluster, but they will not be at exactly the same point every time because of experimental error. That is why you draw the best line or curve you can through the points.
- experimental errors. If your experimental results include graphs, the graphs would be a

good way to show variation in results due to error. Explain the source of these errors and how they might be reduced.

- conclusions you have drawn based on the data you have collected and how you arrived at them.
- a bibliography consisting of any books or magazines you used in your research.

THE SCIENCE FAIR DISPLAY

The display that you make for the fair should be attractive, organized, and possibly colorful. In addition to your report, it would be good to show samples of your data, the plants or animals you used, and your instruments or tools. Examples of your observations and/or results should be part of the display. Judges and visitors might enjoy making a sample run of the experiment you did if that can be arranged practically. Make a good appearance and be prepared to talk knowingly to the judges about your project. Be confident. It's your project, so you probably know more about it than anyone else at the fair.

CONTESTS, INTERNSHIPS, AWARDS, ETC.

Each fair, be it local, state, or national, has its own rules and specifications so read the entry information and application carefully before preparing your presentation.

Ask your teacher for information about state and local science fairs if you are interested in entering one. Listed over are some of the national competitions related to science fairs or research. If you are interested, write for more information.

Earthwatch offers research internships in various science projects throughout the world.

- Earthwatch, 10 Juniper Road, Box 127, Belmont, MA 02178

International Science and Engineering Fair is sponsored by General Motors and nearly fifty other organizations. Projects may be in any of twelve categories ranging from computers to zoology.

- Science Service, 1719 N Street NW, Washington, DC 20036

Jackson Laboratory, Summer Student Program is held every summer in Bar Harbor, Maine. Students work with staff members of the Jackson Laboratory who are engaged in biomedical research.

- Jackson Laboratory, Summer Student Program, Bar Harbor, ME 04609

JETS holds a contest for projects in engineering.

- Junior Engineering Technical Society, 345 East 47th Street, New York, NY 10017

National Science Foundation Science Training Project is a program sponsored by NSF that offers science training at a variety of schools, colleges, and laboratories during the summer months.

- Public Information Branch, National Science Foundation, Washington, DC 20550

NSTA/NASA Space Shuttle Student Involvement Project provides students with an opportunity to propose experiments to be done aboard the Space Shuttle.

- National Science Teachers Association, NSTA/NASA Space Shuttle Student Involvement Project, 1742 Connecticut Avenue, NW, Washington, DC 20009

The Priscilla and Bart Bok Awards are specifically for astronomy projects.

- Prof. Michael D. Papagiannis, Chairman, Dept. of Astronomy, Boston University, Boston, MA 02215

Westinghouse Science Talent Search provides scholarship awards to winners of this program, which involves independent research in the physical, biological, behavioral, and social sciences, as well as in mathematics and engineering.

- Science Service, 1719 N Street NW, Washington, DC 20036

1

GETTING YOUR FEET WET

The projects suggested in this chapter all involve water in one form or another. Some contain fairly detailed instructions about how to do the experiments; some present questions with few if any suggestions as to how you might proceed in answering them. If you have a real flair for scientific investigation and have done a lot of experimenting, you may want to move to these more open-ended projects immediately (unless you find some other experiments along the way that whet your interest). On the other hand, if you're new to the art of inquiry, you may prefer to start with projects that provide more guidance. Later, after you've gotten your feet wet, you may feel more confident about designing your own experiments, equipment, and even your own questions.

HOW BIG ARE RAINDROPS?

You can capture, preserve, and measure raindrops by letting them fall into a pan filled with fine flour that is at least 1 inch (2.5 centimeters, or cm) deep. Each drop will form a tiny pellet of dough. In a normal rainstorm you'll have plenty of samples in just a couple of seconds. After the pellets have dried, you'll be able to measure their diameters with a ruler.

If you're beginning to think like a scientist, you may say, "But the raindrops may not be the same size as the pellets of dough." You're right! But you can let drops of known sizes fall into the flour and then measure the pellets formed. With a variety of eyedroppers, burettes, and drawn glass tubes you can produce water drops of different size.

To measure the volume of a single drop, let several hundred fall into a small graduated cylinder or medicine cup. Then find the volume of a single drop by division. How can you find the diameter of a drop if you know its volume? By making a graph of pellet diameter versus drop diameter you'll be able to find the size of any raindrop from the size of the pellet it made in flour.

In a fine, gentle rain, as long as the drops don't splatter, you can collect droplets on a cookie pan or cardboard sheet covered with waxed paper. Take the pan inside and quickly measure the droplets' diameters with a ruler placed beneath the paper. Or, if the drops are very small, you might want to use a magnifier and ruler to make your measurements. You can see that these drops have become hemispheres on the wax surface. The volume of the hemisphere contains the same amount of water as did the spherical raindrop. How will the diameter of the hemisphere enable you to find the volume of the original raindrop?

As you become skillful at measuring raindrops, you may want to pursue such questions as these: Does the size of the raindrops change as a storm progresses? Are spring raindrops generally larger than those that fall in autumn? Are drops from a shower larger than those from a steady rain? How many raindrops are in a snowflake? A hailstone?

THE SHAPE OF RAINDROPS

Are raindrops really tear-shaped, the way artists draw them? Design an experiment that will enable you to see raindrops as they fall. A good camera may be useful, but raindrops, like all light bodies falling in air, reach a uniform, maximum velocity (called the terminal velocity) after a short time; that is, their speed stops increasing because air resistance becomes equal to the force of gravity. If you could suspend them in midair, you could view them as they appear while falling. A strong, controlled air stream might make this possible.

FALLING DROPS

What does a raindrop look like after it lands? If it falls into water, it produces a "tower." To see what it looks like if it hits a hard surface, use an eyedropper to

A "tower" forms when a drop falls into water.

release drops of colored water above a piece of paper resting on a table or floor. Let the drops fall from different heights. Does the pattern made by the *splashed drop* change as its speed (due to added height of fall) increases?

What happens to the pattern if the drop is moving horizontally as well as vertically? How does the horizontal speed affect the pattern?

Suppose the drop falls on an incline. How will that affect its splash pattern? Design an experiment to find out. Does the steepness of the incline have any effect?

Does the pattern of the *splashed drop* change if the drop lands on different surfaces? Some interesting ones to try are wood, concrete, aluminum foil, and dirt. By all means try waxed paper; it repels water and makes a splash pattern that is quite different than the ones seen on ordinary paper. Can you predict what the pattern will look like?

SAVE A SNOWFLAKE

While you may not have been surprised to learn that raindrops can be captured and measured, you will probably think it impossible to preserve snowflakes. Yet that is exactly what you can do.

To capture the snowflakes, place a number of small glass plates or microscope slides on a flat sheet of wood (a shingle is good) or cardboard. The slides should be placed in a cold, protected place until they are cold. An unheated shed, a freezer, or a covered box will serve the purpose. At the same time, put a spray can of clear lacquer in the same location. The aerosol lacquer Krylon, available in paint and art supply stores, works very well.

After the glass and lacquer have been chilled below the freezing temperature, spray a thin layer of

Snowflakes form in different shapes.

cold lacquer on each piece of glass. Carry the wood or cardboard into the falling snow so that a few flakes collect on each slide. Then put the slides back in the same cold place. Leave them there for several hours until the lacquer is thoroughly dry.

You can bring the dry slides into a warm place and observe the structure of the individual flakes. How many different shapes do you see? What is common to all the flakes? Do different snowstorms produce flakes with distinctly different shapes? Is shape related to temperature? Can you preserve sleet? Can you preserve snowflakes that have already fallen to the ground? Can you preserve the frost patterns that form on windows by spraying the frost with cold lacquer?

ICE KEEPING:
THE ART OF INSULATING

Today it's easy to keep food cold; we simply put it in the refrigerator. But before electricity and refrigerators were common in American households, people stored perishable foods in iceboxes. An icebox was an insulated cabinet that contained a large chunk of ice and space for keeping food. Several times a week an iceman would deliver a large piece of ice to replace the one that was nearly melted.

In the winter large pieces of ice were cut from frozen lakes and ponds. The ice was stored in icehouses, where sawdust was used to cover and insulate it from the heat of summer. These houses had no windows to let in warm sunlight and had roofs so high that warm air would rise and escape through vents. The cold air near the ice caused warmer air to float above it so that hot air never reached the ice. On a hot summer day only swimmers and icemen stayed cool.

You can learn a lot about insulation if you design and build your own mini-icehouses. Identical pieces of ice can be used to test your various ice cube keepers. You can freeze equal volumes of water in identical medicine cups or other containers to be sure the chunks of ice have the same size and shape. The time required for the ice to melt can serve as a means of measuring the effectiveness of the insulating materials.

Sawdust is one insulator that has already been mentioned. You might like to try newspapers, styrofoam, packing materials, or sponges. Another approach would be to suspend the ice on a string in a thermos bottle. You can probably design a number of ingenious icehouses of your own. Which one is the best ice keeper?

MELTING ICE

After you become an expert at insulating ice, you might enjoy investigating the opposite—finding ways to make ice melt faster. For example, does the shape of the ice affect its melting rate? To find out, you could freeze the same volume of water in containers with different shapes. In addition to cube-shaped ice, you could prepare nearly spherical pieces of ice in balloons, ice cones in conical paper cups, cylindrical ice in medicine vials, and wide, short cylinders of ice in the lids from glass jars or plastic containers. Then you can find the time it takes each shape to melt in the same environment. How can you explain your results?

From your investigation of the melting rates of various shapes, can you predict how surface area will affect the rate at which ice melts? What effect do you think stirring or crushing will have on the melting rate?

Does ice melt faster in air or water? To answer this question, you will want to use identical ice cubes and water that has the same temperature as the air around it. How can you suspend the ice so that it does not rest in its own meltwater?

What effect does the amount of water in which an ice cube is placed have on the melting rate? How about the temperature of the water?

THE HEAT TO MELT ICE

Design an experiment to find out how much heat is required to melt 1 gram (g) of ice.

HEAT FLOW AND
SURFACE AREA

If you know how much heat it takes to melt 1 gram of ice, you can calculate the heat needed to melt any mass of the solid. Find out the times required to melt pieces of ice with equal mass but different surface areas. Then you can find out how the rate at which heat flows into the ice is affected by surface area. To keep the difference in temperature between the ice and its surroundings constant, use a large volume of water at room temperature. That way, the water temperature will not be significantly changed by the ice as it melts.

WILL HOT WATER FREEZE FASTER THAN COLD WATER?

You may have heard people say that hot water freezes faster than cold water. After all, at hockey rinks hot water is used to resurface the ice between periods. And some plumbers claim that on very cold days when they are called to repair broken water pipes due to freezing, it is the hot water pipes that freeze first. Does hot water freeze faster than cold water under some (any) conditions?

HUMIDITY: WATER IN THE AIR

You can't see the water that's dissolved in air, but if you breathe on a cold window, you'll see the moisture in your exhaled air condensing on the glass. Similarly, on a cold winter morning you can see moisture that has condensed and frozen to form frost on a window pane.

The solubility of sugar in water increases with temperature; so does the solubility of moisture in air. When a certain volume of water holds as much sugar as can be dissolved at a given temperature, we say the solution is saturated. The same is true of the solution formed when water dissolves in air. The chart on the next page gives the saturation points, in one cubic meter of air, for several temperatures. More extensive tables can be found in chemistry or physics handbooks or in books on weather.

Temperature (°C)	Grams of water per cubic meter of air
0 (32°F)	4.8
5 (41°F)	6.8
10 (50°F)	9.3
15 (59°F)	12.7
20 (68°F)	17.1
25 (77°F)	22.8
30 (86°F)	30.0
35 (95°F)	39.2

The mass of water dissolved in 1 cubic meter of air is called the *absolute humidity*. You can determine the absolute humidity by finding the dew point—the temperature at which moisture begins to condense from the air.

Put some warm water in a shiny metal can. Add small pieces of ice to the water as you stir it with a thermometer. (Be careful not to breathe on the can.) Record the temperature at which you first see moisture condensing on the shiny surface. That temperature is the dew point.

Suppose you first see moisture when the can's temperature is 15°C. Then the air is saturated with moisture at 15°C. At 15°C there are 12.7 g of water in each cubic meter of air. The absolute humidity is therefore 12.7 grams per cubic meter (g/m^3). If the temperature of the air is 25°C, the air could hold as much as 22.8 g/m^3. The ratio of the absolute humidity to the maximum amount of water vapor that the air could hold per cubic meter if it were saturated is called the *relative humidity*. It is usually expressed as a percent. In this case the relative humidity is 12.7/ 22.8=0.557=55.7 percent.

Now that you know how to find absolute and relative humidity, you can investigate the humidity of the air inside and outside your home or school during different seasons of the year. How does the humidity inside compare with the humidity outside? How do your humidity measurements compare on clear, cloudy, and rainy days? Do humidifiers really increase the water content of the air in a home? Can you measure the effect of a dehumidifier? What is a sling psychrometer? Can you build one? How could you use it to measure relative humidity?

CLIMBING WATER:
A WAY TO DEFY GRAVITY

Paper towels can be used to clean up water spills. But why does water soak into paper? If you look at a piece of paper towel or blotter paper under a microscope, you will see tiny spaces between the wood fibers that make up the paper. Water is attracted to the fibers, and these forces of attraction cause water to rise up the narrow channels until counterbalanced by the weight of the water. Put two glass plates together as shown in Figure 1. You will see the water rise higher as the opening becomes narrower. How high will water "climb" in a paper towel?

Cut a piece of paper towel or blotter paper about 1 inch (2.5 cm) wide by a foot (30 cm) long. Use a piece of tape to hang the strip from a cabinet, chair, or table so that one of the narrow ends dips into some colored water. (Use a few drops of food coloring.) After several hours you will see that the water has climbed partway up the towel. How high will the water rise?

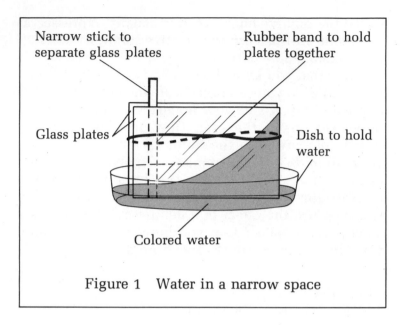

Narrow stick to separate glass plates

Rubber band to hold plates together

Glass plates

Dish to hold water

Colored water

Figure 1   Water in a narrow space

Repeat the experiment, but this time use several strips of different widths, from ⅛ inch to 2 inches (0.3 cm to 5 cm). Does the width of the strip affect the height to which the water rises?

To help you explain these results, repeat the experiment using two identical strips of paper. Cover all but the bottoms of the strips with plastic tubing or waxed paper. (You can seal the edges of the waxed paper together with tape to make a tubelike structure.) In which paper strip, covered or uncovered, does water rise higher? Why do you think this happens?

You can also try the experiment using strips of different kinds of paper, cloth, string, blotters, balsa wood, and other materials that you think might work. What do you find? How do you explain your results?

To see if some liquids are more attracted to wood fibers than others, try the experiment using such liquids as alcohol, cooking oil, soapy water, and saltwater as well as plain water.

IS "BOUNTY" REALLY BETTER?

You've probably seen ads telling you that Bounty-brand towels are better than other paper towels. Is this true? Design experiments that will enable you to compare Bounty towels with other brands. Is Bounty really a "better picker-upper?"

STREAM TABLES: A MODEL FOR STUDYING WATER FLOW AND EROSION

If your school has a stream table, you may be able to use it to investigate the effects of water flow and speed on various soils, the formation of deltas, the movement of beaches, and various other earth-water interactions that are of interest to you. If you don't have access to a stream table, you can build one as shown in Figure 2.

HOW THICK IS A SOAP BUBBLE?

We all enjoy blowing soap bubbles, and we know the bubbles are very thin. But how thin are they? See if you can figure out several ways to measure their thickness. Your various methods should all give similar values. Once you get into your investigation, you will see the colors in the bubbles. What causes the colors? What do the colors indicate about bubble thickness?

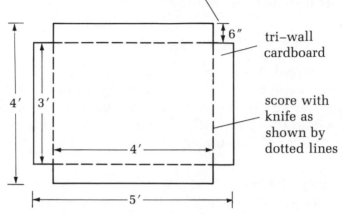

Cut 6–inch (15–cm) square from each corner

6″ — tri–wall cardboard

score with knife as shown by dotted lines

4′ 3′ 4′

5′

Fold cardboard to form box 3 ft × 4 ft × 0.5 ft
(0.9 × 1.2 × 0.2 m). Use heavy waterproof tape to
secure corners. Line box with heavy duty plastic sheet.

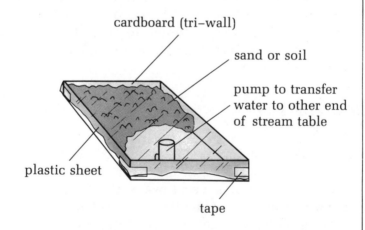

cardboard (tri–wall)

sand or soil

pump to transfer
water to other end
of stream table

plastic sheet

tape

Figure 2   How to build a stream table

WHY DOES A TOY
DRINKING BIRD DRINK?

It's fascinating to watch a toy drinking (or dipping) bird (see Figure 3) "drink" at regular intervals for hours on end. But why does the bird drink? To understand the bird's behavior, you'll find it instructive to investigate the factors that control the *rate* at which the bird dips its beak into the water (or other liquids).

cloth–covered head

tube connecting bulb at head with bulb at tail

liquid that rises from lower to upper bulb

water or other liquid

legs that serve as a stand for bird to swing on

Figure 3   A toy drinking (or dipping) bird

2

ASTRONOMY

Don't leave this chapter just because you don't have a telescope. You can do a lot of astronomy without looking through a lens or into a mirror.

One important caution for all astronomical observations: **Never look directly at the sun, even through an optical device! The light is so bright that it can do serious damage to your eyes.**

WHICH WAY IS NORTH?

If you live in the continental United States or Canada, you see the sun rise, ascend into the southern sky, and set along the western horizon. You will never see the sun directly overhead or in the northern sky at midday, but you will see the sun reach its zenith (maximum altitude) in the southern sky at that time. Because the sun is due south at midday you can easily establish which direction is true north.

Look at the shadow of a vertical stick late in the morning. Place a marker at the end of the stick's shadow. Using the distance between the stick and the end of its shadow as a radius, draw a circle around the stick. Watch the shadow shorten, then mark the direction of the shadow when it is shortest. What is the direction of this shadow? To confirm your measurement, continue to watch the shadow until its end again lies on the circle you drew. Mark this point. Now draw a line connecting the two marks. A line from the stick to the midpoint of the line you just drew should be in the direction of the shadow when it was shortest. Why?

Does midday according to the sun always occur at noon according to the clock? Why do sun time and clock time differ?

To further confirm that you have established the direction of true north, see if the line that you have made points toward a point directly beneath the north star (Polaris). Figure 4 will help you find Polaris. The Big Dipper is easy to find in the northern sky. Its two pointer stars, Dubhe and Merak, are nearly aligned with the north star. With your hand at arm's length, place two fingers on the pointer stars. Polaris will be about five times the distance between the pointer stars along the direction established by Dubhe and Merak. Does the direction north indicated by the stick's shortest shadow fall under the north star?

Why can't you use a compass needle to find true north in most places?

WATCHING THE
NORTHERN SKY

Now that you know how to find true north, you might enjoy watching the stars in the vicinity of Polaris. You can easily identify the constellations shown in Figure 4. Observe them at different times of the night from early evening to dawn. Do their positions in the sky change?

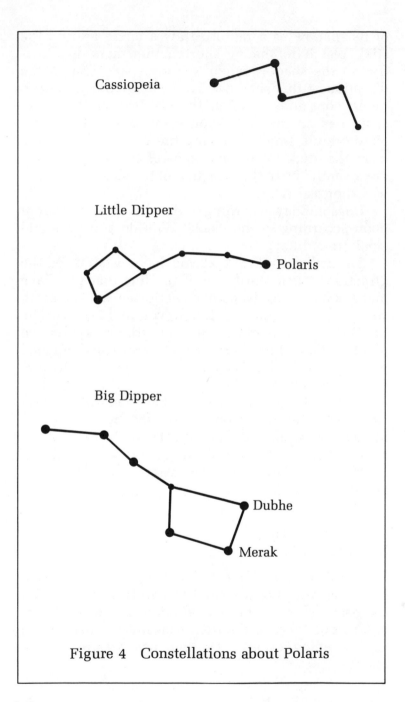

Figure 4   Constellations about Polaris

Watch these same constellations from season to season. Are their positions in the sky always the same at the same time of day?

Try to explain your observations about these stars in terms of earth's motion through space.

If you enjoy watching stars, you will probably want to identify other constellations and observe their paths through the heavens. Not all the constellations are visible every clear night. Some are visible only during certain seasons of the year. Again, try to explain why some constellations are often hidden from view, while others can be seen every clear night.

MAPPING THE SUN

Look up at the sky on a clear day when you are standing in a large open space. You are at the center of what appears to be a huge blue hemisphere. At night, stars glisten like tiny lights set in the surface of this now darkened dome. Astronomers call this dome a *celestial hemisphere*. The other half of the sky would be seen by someone standing on the other side of earth. The two hemispheres make up the *celestial sphere*. Stars and planets appear to follow paths along the celestial hemisphere.

One star's path through the sky is easy to map; that's our nearest star, the sun. To establish the path of the sun across the sky, you will need a clear plastic dome and a marking pen. Put the dome on a piece of white paper resting on a flat board or a sheet of cardboard. Draw a circle around the base of the dome; then remove the dome and make a mark at the very center of the circle. Replace the dome and tape it to the board. Place the dome in a level place where it will be in sunlight all day.

The dot at the center of the circle represents you; the dome represents the sky, or celestial hemisphere.

To map the sun's path, start as soon after sunrise as possible. Place the tip of the marking pen on the clear dome so that the shadow of the tip cast by the sun falls on the mark at the center of the circle you drew. Mark that point on the dome with your pen. As you see in Figure 5, this pen mark represents the position of the sun in the sky. How do you know the mark is in line with the center mark and the sun?

Continue to make marks like this every hour or half hour throughout the day. By evening you will

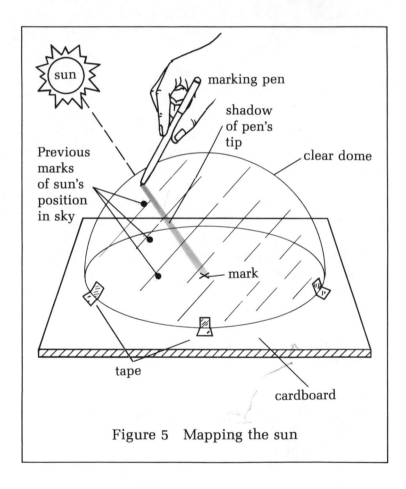

Figure 5   Mapping the sun

have a pattern that maps the sun's path along the celestial hemisphere.

If you mark north on this dome, you can use it to map the sun's path across the sky at various times during the year. Or you can use a different dome each time. Try to map the sun's path at the beginning of each season. What dates mark the start of spring, summer, autumn, and winter? How does the sun's path along the sky change from season to season?

By using your solar maps and by observing shadows at sunrise and sunset, try to determine the direction of sunrise and sunset at various times of the year. Does the sun always rise in the east and set in the west? When is sunrise due east? Try to explain why the sun's position in the sky changes during the year. You might make a model of earth and sun using a ball and a light bulb in a large, dark room.

MOON MAPPING
AND WATCHING

The moon's path across the sky is more difficult to map because the moon casts less distinct shadows and is often seen in the daytime sky. With an astrolabe, like the one in Figure 6, you can determine the moon's altitude at various times of the night or day. Also, you can observe its rising and setting positions along the horizon. (Telescopic observations of the moon are interesting too.)

As with the sun, map the moon's path across the sky over a year's time. You will see that the moon's shape undergoes periodic and predictable changes. Collect as much data as you can every day. Why does the moon's path change so much faster than the sun's?

How do you explain the changes in the moon's appearance and celestial path? A model of the sun, moon, and earth may help you explain your data.

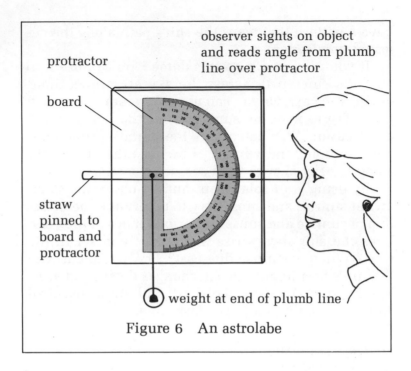

observer sights on object
and reads angle from plumb
line over protractor

protractor

board

straw
pinned to
board and
protractor

weight at end of plumb line

Figure 6   An astrolabe

THE SIZE OF THE
SUN AND MOON

Use a pin to make a tiny hole in the center of a piece of
black construction paper. If you let sunlight pass
through the hole onto a white screen held near the
black paper, you will see a pinhole image of the sun.
To prove to yourself that it really is an image, move
the screen closer to and farther from the pinhole.
What happens to the size of the image? Cut a tiny
square and triangle in the same black paper. Do these
holes also produce round images? Why does a tiny
pinhole produce an image of the sun? Can you make
pinhole images of other light sources such as a candle
flame or a light bulb?

Once you've explained why pinhole images form,
see if you can use a pinhole image to measure the

diameter of the sun, knowing that the sun is 96 million miles (154 million kilometers, or km) from earth.

With a full moon you might be able to use the same method to measure the moon's diameter; however, since you can look directly at the moon, matching the moon's diameter with the diameter of an object held a known distance from your eye will allow you to use similar triangles to find the diameter of the moon, which is about 240,000 miles (386,000 km) from earth.

A GLOBAL VIEW OF EARTH

Place a large globe of the earth outside in a location where it will be in sunlight all day. A large empty can will provide good support for the globe, as shown in Figure 7. Arrange the globe so that it represents the way you see the earth, that is, with your location at the very top of the globe. Then turn the globe so that its north pole points at Polaris. As long as your hometown is at the very top of the globe, why will the globe's north pole automatically be directed toward Polaris when the globe's poles are along a north-south axis?

Use a bit of clay to hold a pin vertically at the top of the globe. The pin represents you, and its shadow on the globe should be parallel to yours on the ground.

The globe provides a view of what earth would look like from far out in space. From this special view, where on earth is the sun rising right now? Where is the sun setting? Where is it dark? Are there places, near one of the poles, where the sun will not rise at all today? Are there places, near the other pole, where the sun will never set today? What time is it now in Chicago? San Francisco? Honolulu? Oslo? Peking? Tokyo? Athens?

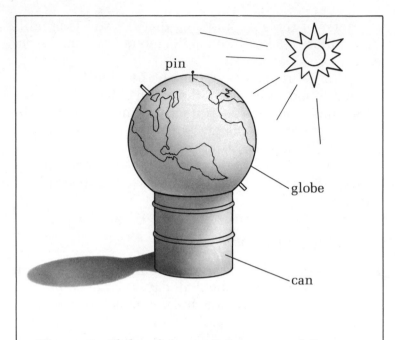

Figure 7   If the globe can't be removed from its stand, tilt the entire structure and support it

A perpendicular object will not cast a shadow if the sun is directly overhead. Use a short piece of soda straw with a pin through it to locate a place on earth where the sun is directly overhead right now. Try to predict where on earth the sun will be directly overhead 1 hour from now. Test your prediction an hour later. Were you right?

Watch the globe throughout the day. What happens to the western parts of the globe that are near the edge of darkness as the day progresses?

Using a ball to represent the moon, find out where the moon is relative to the earth and sun so that it has the appearance it has today. Where is the moon relative to you, the earth, and the sun when it is full? when it is a new moon?

Repeat your global observations at different times of the year. What changes do you notice?

What else can you learn from this global view of earth?

A SIMPLE TELESCOPE

Use a pair of lenses and some mail tubing to build a simple telescope. Find the focal length of each lens. Arrange the lenses relative to their focal lengths to get the greatest magnification. Determine the magnification of your telescope.

ENERGY OF THE PYRAMIDS

Some people claim that pyramids are able to store some kind of energy because of their shape. They claim that food stored in a pyramid will decay more slowly than in other places; that razor blades retain their sharpness or even get sharper if kept within a pyramid; and that by sleeping within or beneath a pyramid one can acquire additional energy and success. Design experiments to test these claims about pyramids. You can buy ready-made pyramids for this purpose from Edmund Scientific Company, 101 E. Gloucester Pike, Barrington, NJ 08007.

COUNTING STARS

When you look up at the sky on a clear, cold night, millions of stars appear to be in the sky. But how many can you really see?

To estimate the number of visible stars, count the stars in sample areas of the sky and then multiply to find the number expected for the entire area of the celestial hemisphere.

Cut a square 4 inches (10 cm) on a side from the center of a large cardboard sheet. Hold the sheet exactly 1 foot (30 cm) in front of your eye. Keeping your head very still, count all the distinct stars you can see through the square hole in the sheet. The area through which you view the stars is 1/57th of the total area; therefore, if you multiply the number of stars you counted by 57, you should have the total number of stars visible in the celestial hemisphere.

Why is the area of the sky that you are viewing 1/57th of the total area of the celestial hemisphere? Would it be better to make several counts of the stars through the square while viewing different parts of the sky and take an average before multiplying by 57?

Count the number of visible stars. Would you find more or fewer visible stars if the sky were hazy? If you looked through a telescope? If you included the Milky Way?

THE ART OF ESTIMATING

When you counted the stars in the sky, you used a technique of estimating. The art of estimating is an important one in science because often we want to know the number of something that is too big to count one by one.

See if you can devise estimating techniques to find the number of: blades of grass in a lawn, beans in a large jar, leaves on a tree, hot dogs eaten in the United States in one year, molecules in a glass of water, and other numbers that require the practical art of estimating, such as the amount of paint to cover your house, the weight of grass seed to plant a lawn, and the squares of shingles to cover your roof.

3

LET THE LIGHT
SHINE IN

Light is essential to our existence, not only because most objects are visible solely from the light
they reflect, but because without light, plants could
not manufacture food. Many people live without
being able to see, but no one can live without food.

WHERE IS YOUR IMAGE?

Look into a plane mirror. Where does your image
appear to be? Wink your right eye. Which eye does
your image wink? Raise your right hand. Which hand
does your image raise?

To locate a mirror image, you can draw sight lines.
To see that this method really works, draw some sight
lines to a real object.

Place a sheet of paper on a piece of cardboard.
Stick a large pin or a nail in the center of the paper.
With a pair of common pins at arm's length, establish
a line of sight to the large pin or nail from your eye as
shown in Figure 8. Make several other sight lines to
the pin or nail in the same way. Use a ruler placed

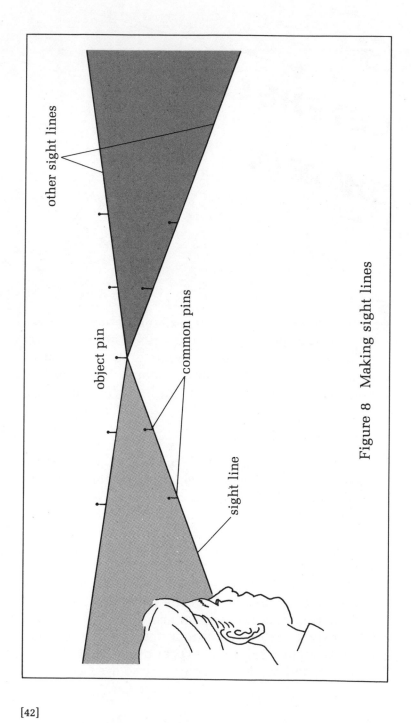

other sight lines

object pin

common pins

sight line

Figure 8   Making sight lines

against the pins and a pencil to mark the lines. Do the sight lines meet at the nail or pin? Can we assume that light travels in straight lines? Find other methods to show that light travels in straight lines.

Use the same method to locate the position of an image in a mirror. Place the same large pin or a nail in front of a mirror. Mark the front or back of the mirror with a pencil line on a sheet of paper. (A piece of clay can be used to support the mirror.) Use pins to establish several sight lines to the image. Be sure you are sighting on the image seen in the mirror, not the actual pin or nail. Remove the mirror and draw the sight lines. Where do they meet? What does this tell you about the location of images seen in a plane mirror? How does the distance of the image from the mirror compare with the distance of the object (pin or nail) from the mirror? See if you can predict the position of the image when the object is in front of, but to one side of the mirror. Before you check up on your prediction, here is an easier way to locate an image; it involves something called *parallax*.

When two objects are aligned, but at different distances from you, the closer one will seem to move back and forth across the farther one when you move your head from side to side. This apparent motion of one object relative to another because of differences in distance is called parallax. A tree, for example, shows parallax relative to a distant mountain. However, if two things are at the same place they will show no evidence of parallax. Prove this to yourself by looking at two pencils and shifting your head; first, when the pencils are at different distances from your eye, and then when they are at the same position.

Use parallax to locate the position of an image seen in a mirror. Place a mirror on a sheet of cardboard. Stick a nail or pin upright in front of the mirror. Next, place a pencil or long nail behind the mirror.

This object should be taller than the mirror. Move the object around until it and the image show no parallax. You will then know that the image and the nail or pencil behind the mirror are at the same place. You might like to try this method first when you know the position of the image. A pencil or pin taller than the mirror can be used to locate the image. Once you've mastered the parallax method, use it to test the prediction you made earlier. See Figure 9.

Why are mirror images found where they are? Think about how light from an object gets to your eye. It must first strike the mirror and then follow a path to your eye. Repeat your sight line method for locating an image in a mirror. Draw the sight lines. Then draw the path that each light ray must have followed in traveling from the object to the mirror before being reflected to your eye. Measure the angle between the incident ray (the light ray to the mirror) and the mirror. Also measure the angle between the reflected ray

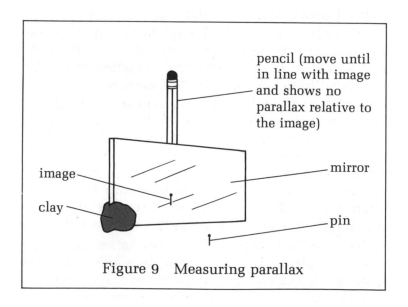

Figure 9   Measuring parallax

and the mirror. Do this for each of the sight lines. How do these two angles compare in each case? Now can you explain why images are seen where they are?

Use what you have learned about reflection and images to write some words that can be read correctly only by placing a mirror on the paper above the words. This is called mirror writing.

Place two plane mirrors with their reflecting surfaces at right angles. Put an object midway between the mirrors. How many images do you see? What happens to the number of images as you reduce the angle between the mirrors? Find a relationship between the number of images seen and the angle that lies between the reflecting surfaces. How many images are visible when the mirrors are parallel?

A STRANGE REFLECTION: SQUARE TO CIRCLE

Use a square or rectangular mirror to reflect a beam of sunlight. Hold a screen close to the mirror. The reflected beam forms a square patch of light on the screen. But what happens to the size and shape of the light patch as you move the screen farther from the mirror? Look at the light patch on the side of a building 100 or 200 feet (30 or 60 m) away. What shape is the reflected patch? Why?

CURVED MIRRORS

Not all mirrors are flat. A shaving or makeup mirror has a concave shape like a saucer. The side mirrors on some trucks and cars or the mirrors in many stores are convex. They have a slight domelike shape.

A concave mirror, as you might expect, will bring parallel rays of light together. In fact, if you hold a concave mirror some distance from a window, you can form an image of what you see through the window on a white sheet of cardboard held in front of, and slightly to one side of the mirror. Move the screen back and forth until the image is clear. Unlike images formed in a plane mirror, these images are actually on the screen. That is why they are called *real images*, and that is why you can "capture" them on a screen. You certainly can't do that with the images seen in a plane mirror; that's why those images are called *virtual images*. But why is the real image upside down? Is it also reversed right for left?

A *focal length* is defined as that distance from the concave mirror at which parallel rays of light are brought together. Since the rays of light from a point on a distant object that reach a concave mirror must be nearly parallel, the point where the rays come together (forming an image) is nearly 1 focal length from the mirror. The point where these rays meet is called the *principal focus* of the mirror. Why are the rays from a distant object that strike the mirror almost parallel?

Find the focal length of your concave mirror. Then place a small lighted bulb such as a flashlight bulb at a position greater than 1 focal length from the reflecting surface of the mirror (Figure 10). Where is the image of the bulb found? What happens to the image position if you move the bulb 2 focal lengths from the mirror? 3 focal lengths? 4? still farther?

Now place the bulb between the principal focus and the mirror. Start at a position ½ focal length from the mirror. Where is the image now? Since you can't find a real image, use the parallax method to locate the image. What happens to the image as the object (light bulb) is moved closer to the mirror? Farther from the mirror (but still less than 1 focal length)?

Now investigate the image positions of an object seen in a concave mirror. How do the position and size of these images change as the object is moved?

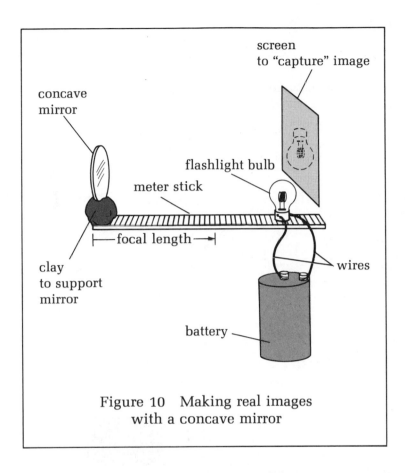

concave mirror

screen to "capture" image

flashlight bulb

meter stick

├─focal length─┤

clay to support mirror

wires

battery

Figure 10   Making real images with a concave mirror

To understand the images formed by plane, concave, and convex mirrors, you might like to design and build a ray maker or light box like the one shown in Figure 11. With it you can make light rays and see what happens to them when they strike plane mirrors and two-dimensional concave and convex reflecting surfaces. In fact, as the drawing shows, you can make images from the light rays emitted by an object.

From what you have learned, see if you can form some mathematical relationships among object distance, image distance, focal length, object size, and

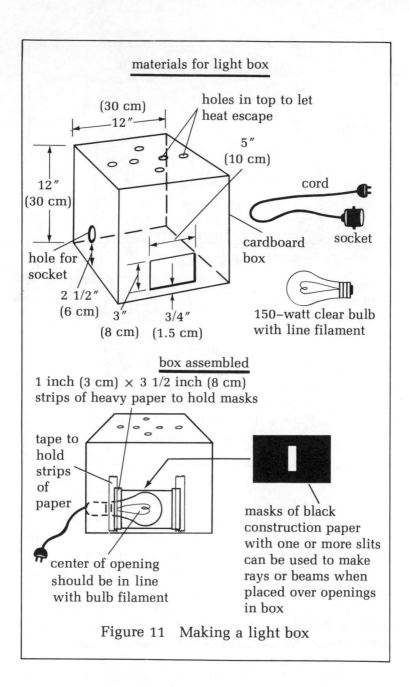

materials for light box

(30 cm)
12″

holes in top to let
heat escape

5″
(10 cm)

12″
(30 cm)

cord

socket

hole for
socket

cardboard
box

2 1/2″
(6 cm)   3″   3/4″
        (8 cm)   (1.5 cm)

150–watt clear bulb
with line filament

box assembled

1 inch (3 cm) × 3 1/2 inch (8 cm)
strips of heavy paper to hold masks

tape to
hold
strips
of
paper

masks of black
construction paper
with one or more slits
can be used to make
rays or beams when
placed over openings
in box

center of opening
should be in line
with bulb filament

Figure 11   Making a light box

image size for concave and, perhaps, convex mirrors.

BENDING LIGHT

Use a bit of clay to support a plane mirror on white paper over cardboard. Mark the front or rear edge of the mirror so that it can be replaced if accidentally moved. Use two pins to establish a line (ray) of light to the mirror. To mark the reflected ray, place two more pins in line with the images of the first two pins as shown in Figure 12a. Use a ruler and pencil to mark the rays of light. You now have an incident ray (going to the mirror) and a reflected ray (coming from the mirror). How does the angle between the incident ray and mirror surface compare with the angle between the reflected ray and the mirror? Is this true for all incident and reflected rays?

Now that you know how to make incident and reflected rays, repeat the experiment but this time let the light reflect from the mirror *after* passing through water, plastic, or glass (Figure 12b). Remove the water or transparent block and again draw the incident and reflected rays as established by the sighting pins. Where do these rays meet? Could the reflection have taken place in *front* of the mirror? How do you explain these results? Design an experiment to test your hypothesis. You might find the light box in Figure 11 useful in your experiment.

SIMPLE MICROSCOPES

Use a pair of convex lenses to build a simple microscope. Should one lens have a shorter focal length than the other? See if you can figure out how these lenses work to create a magnified image. You might

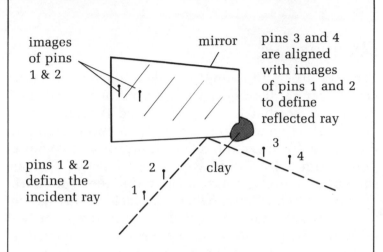

images
of pins
1 & 2

mirror

pins 3 and 4
are aligned
with images
of pins 1 and 2
to define
reflected ray

3

4

pins 1 & 2
define the
incident ray

2

1

clay

Figure 12a   Mapping light rays with pins

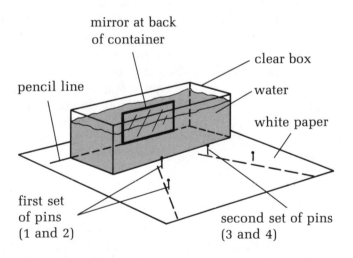

mirror at back
of container

clear box

pencil line

water

white paper

first set
of pins
(1 and 2)

second set of pins
(3 and 4)

Figure 12b   A setup for finding where incident
and reflected rays meet

take a look at a commercial microscope to see how it is built.

Try making a simple microscope using a drop of water as a lens. Try other liquids. Which liquid works best?

CYLINDRICAL LENSES
AND TRIANGULAR PRISMS

Jars and vials of water can serve as two-dimensional models of lenses. With a light box to create rays and a cylinder of water to serve as a lens, you can investigate the way convex lenses form images. You can even change the amount that the light is bent by adding sugar to the water.

Here's a fun experiment that you can try on your friends once you figure it out. Fill two large plastic pill bottles with hot water. Add a drop of blue food coloring to one and a drop of red food coloring to the other. On a piece of paper write the words "OXIDE" and "SPACE." Place the blue vial horizontally over the word "OXIDE." Slowly raise the vial until you get a clear image. Use the red vial to view the word "SPACE." Is either word inverted? If so, why is one word inverted and not the other? Is it because of the color of the water?

If you let a ray of light enter a glass or plastic prism, you can expect it to refract the light, but you may be surprised to find that it bends some colors more than others. Which colored light is refracted the most? Which color is refracted least? Is there a similar effect with lenses? With cylindrical lenses? Look carefully. Would this difference in the way different colors are refracted have any effect on the focal length of different colors of light? How might it affect our perception of depth? Do artists use this effect in trying to create depth in two-dimensional paintings?

MIRAGES, REFLECTION, AND REFRACTION

Many mirages, such as the apparent presence of water on a hot paved road, inverted ships on the sea, or pools of water in the desert, are the result of reflection and/ or refraction. Try to observe a number of mirages. Can you explain these mirages using what you know about reflection and refraction of light?

MIXING COLORED LIGHTS

Using mirrors, a light box, and a cover that transmits beams of red, blue, and green light (Figure 13), you can mix colored light. (Good colored filters can be obtained from Rosco Laboratories, Inc., 36 Bush Avenue, Port Chester, NY 10573. Order medium red #823, medium blue #863, and medium green #874.) Use a mirror to reflect red light onto a green light beam viewed on white paper. You will find that the mixture is yellow. Red and blue light produce magenta, and green and blue give cyan. Try to make white light from these colored beams.

Place a pencil near the light box so that it casts a shadow along one of the light beams. What could you do to give part of the shadow a yellow color? A cyan color? A magenta color? Try to give the shadow colored stripes. Where have you seen colored shadows before?

When you think you understand the mixing of colored light, cover the stage of each of three overhead projectors with a piece of cardboard. At the center of each cardboard sheet, cut a circular opening 3 to 4 inches (8 to 10 cm) in diameter. Cover each opening with a sheet of different colored plastic—red, blue, and green—so that you can shine circles of the primary colors on a white screen. You should be able to predict the color of your hand's shadow when held in any

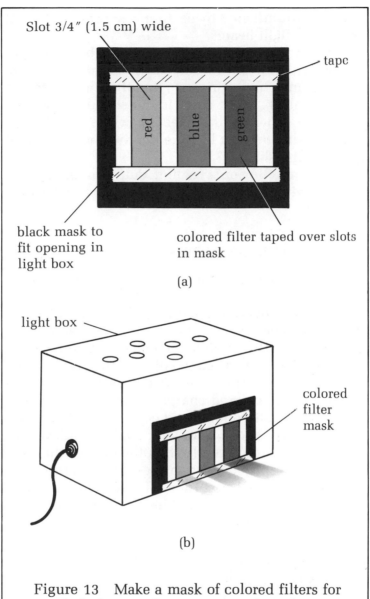

Slot 3/4″ (1.5 cm) wide

tapc

red

blue

green

black mask to
fit opening in
light box

colored filter taped over slots
in mask

(a)

light box

colored
filter
mask

(b)

Figure 13   Make a mask of colored filters for
your light box as shown in (a). Place the mask
over an opening in the box.

beam and illuminated by each or any combination of the colored light beams.

Suppose you hold your hand in a red beam of light casting a shadow on the screen illuminated by *white* light. You may be surprised to find that the shadow is cyan, not black. What color is the shadow cast by a green light when illuminated by white light? How about the shadow cast by blue light when white light shines on the shadow?

Is this an illusion? To find out, photograph the shadows with color film. What do you find? Explain this effect.

INVESTIGATING SHADOWS

Not all shadows are colored, but they are all usually interesting.

Watch shadows change during the course of a day. Watch the shadows of poles, buildings, and other objects change their midday length during the course of a year. Watch the direction of morning and evening shadows change from season to season. See where shadows are fuzzy and sharp. See how they change when cast by different lights. Look for multiple shadows, for funny shadows, for overlapping shadows, for shadows shaped differently than the objects that cast them. Photograph shadows and see if people can identify the objects that cast them. There's no end to an investigation of shadows or the questions that your observations will raise.

COLORED OBJECTS
IN COLORED LIGHT

A blue object is blue because it reflects only blue light; it absorbs other colors such as green and red. Why then is an object yellow? magenta? cyan? black?

white? To check up on your hypothesis, see if you can predict what color various small pieces of colored construction paper will appear to have when viewed in light of different colors.

PINHOLE IMAGES

Cover an opening in a light box with a piece of black construction paper. Use a pin to punch a tiny hole in the paper. Now hold a white screen near the hole. You should see an image of the light bulb's filament. What happens to the size of the image as you move the screen farther from the box. Explain this image. Is it inverted? Is it turned right for left? How can you find out?

What happens if you punch a second hole in the paper? What effect does the size of the pinhole have on the image?

Using a large box, you can use the pinhole method to make a good sized image of the sun that you can view in semidarkness. See if you can make the image large enough to see sunspots.

MAKING RAINBOWS

A diffraction grating is a piece of glass or plastic with many very fine parallel scratches. Some of the white light passing through the narrow slits between the scratches is separated into a spectrum that reveals all the colors that make up white light.

With the large box that you used to make a pinhole image of the sun, mount a diffraction grating over a small opening cut in one end of the box near the top. At the other end of the box, on each side of the square patch of light that comes straight through the grating, you will see a rainbow-like spectrum, made from the sun's white light passing through the grating. Can you see a similar "rainbow" using the grating and a light box? Try to explain why light passing through the grating creates a spectrum.

Using prisms, mirrors, bubble makers, vessels of water, garden hoses, and sunlight, see how many different ways you can make rainbows. Then try to explain how a natural rainbow is made.

Diffraction grating material can be obtained from Edmund Scientific, 101 E. Gloucester Pike, Barrington, NJ 08007.

BUILD A SPECTROMETER

A spectrometer is a device that can be used to separate light according to its wavelength. See if you can find out how to measure the wavelength of light with a spectrometer. Then build your own spectrometer using a diffraction grating, a light source, a box, measuring tape, and other materials you find useful.

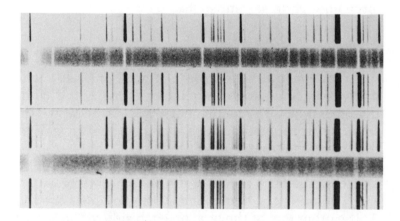

Section of spectra of a star. The lines correspond to different wavelengths of light produced by the burning of different elements.

CAN LIGHT BE BENT
WITH MAGNETS?

You've seen that light can be bent off its normal straight-line path using water, glass, or a diffraction grating. Do you think a strong magnetic field will deflect a light beam? To find out, let a narrow beam of light, such as a laser beam, pass between the poles of a strong magnet. Mark the position of the light on a distant screen, then remove and replace the magnet. Is light deflected by the magnet?

When you use a laser, be sure to follow these safety rules because laser light can be harmful to human eyes.

- **Never look into the laser beam.**
- **Do not look at laser light reflected from a shiny surface. Even reflected laser light can be dangerous.**
- **Do not let the laser light pass through windows where it might accidentally strike someone's eye.**
- **Lock the door or post a warning outside the room where you are experimenting so that no one entering the room runs the danger of having laser light enter his or her eye.**

PHOTOGRAPHING LIGHTNING

To capture the beautiful zigzag pattern of lightning flashes, set up a camera on a tripod in a room where you can see lightning through a window at night. Turn off all inside lights and aim the camera at the active clouds. After several minutes, you'll develop a feel for when the next flash will occur. Set the camera at f16 and focus on infinity. Anticipate the stroke by a few seconds and make 20- to 30-second time exposures.

4

CHEMISTRY

Chemistry is concerned with the structure of matter and the way different kinds of matter combine or decompose. It is an exciting part of science, but it can also be very dangerous. Before proceeding with the projects in this chapter, read the following paragraph *and* the safety information on page 9.

Always do chemistry experiments under supervision of a knowledgeable adult (like your science teacher) and in an environment conducive to safety. ALWAYS WEAR SAFETY GOGGLES WHILE PERFORMING CHEMISTRY EXPERIMENTS. On Experiments that don't involve chemicals, *check with your science teacher or another adult even if the experiment looks as if it doesn't have to be done under supervision.* **You can never be too careful when doing chemistry experiments.**

HOW MUCH OXYGEN IS THERE IN AIR?

Some books tell us that the following experiment can be done to find out what fraction of the air is oxygen.

Use a small lump of clay to hold a birthday candle upright in a shallow dish of water. When the candle has burned for several minutes, cover it with a tall, narrow glass jar such as the kind olives come in. Measure the height to which the water rises after the candle goes out. How does the height of the water level compare with the total height of the jar? The ratio of these two heights will give you the fraction of the air that is oxygen.

Try this experiment for yourself. Repeat it a few times. Do you get the same results each time? Put a little soap in the water and notice the bubbles that form when you place the jar over the candle. What do you think causes the bubbles?

Here is another way to measure the percentage of oxygen in air. Place a small loosely rolled ball of steel wool in a solution of vinegar (one part vinegar to two parts water). Let it soak overnight to remove the protective coating on the steel. Shake off the excess liquid and push the steel ball to the bottom of a tall jar like the ones that olives come in. Invert the jar in a dish of shallow, colored water so that the mouth of the jar is below the water level. Leave this set up for 24 hours. What happens? Leave it for another day to see if there are further changes. Look at the steel wool carefully. What has happened?

According to this experiment, what fraction of the air is oxygen? Repeat the experiment several times. Are the results consistent? What causes water to rise in the jar? Which method *really* measures the percentage of oxygen in air? What evidence do you have to support your decision? Carry out any additional experiments that help to support your position.

WEIGHING GASES

Weigh an empty plastic bag and a tie band. Fill the bag with air, tie it shut with the tie band, and reweigh it.

How much does the air appear to weigh? Why? If you have trouble explaining your result, ask yourself this question: How much do you weigh when you float in water?

Invent a method that will allow you to weigh air and other gases.

Once you've found a way to weigh gases, see if you can predict the results of this experiment. Place some water in the bottom of a long balloon. Use a tie band to seal the water off from the rest of the balloon. Pour some Bromo-seltzer or pieces of Alka-seltzer into the upper part of the balloon above the water. Tie off the top of the balloon and hang it from one end of a sensitive balance. If you now remove the tie band that separates the seltzer from the water and attach it to the top of the balloon, the seltzer will fall into the water. What will happen? Will the apparent mass of the balloon and its contents increase, decrease, or remain the same?

IDENTIFYING METALS

Collect a number of metal samples. They should be of reasonable size—10 cm³ or more. You will also need a

Crystals of the metal bismuth (left) and a model of crystalline structure (right)

reference table that gives the properties of various metals. You can find such information in a handbook of chemistry and physics or in physics and chemistry textbooks.

Find the density and specific heat of each metal. With that information can you identify all of the metals? If not, what additional information would be helpful?

SEPARATING A MIXTURE

Add the following substances to a jar: 50 milliliters (ml) of water, 25 ml of methyl alcohol, some sand, some charcoal, a teaspoon of salt, and a couple of drops of black ink or food coloring. Stir the mixture.

Design a method for separating the components of this mixture. **Explain the method to your science teacher or another knowledgeable adult and ask permission to begin your experimental work.**

TITRATING HOUSEHOLD LIQUIDS

The vinegar and ammonia that you buy in a store are both on the order of 1 molar* (1M) in concentration; that is, they contain 1 mole of the solute (acetic acid or ammonia) per liter. Using standardized solutions of sodium hydroxide and hydrochloric acid, as well as appropriate indicators and burettes, determine the actual concentration of acetic acid in vinegar and the concentration of ammonia in household ammonia. Does the concentration of acid in the vinegar agree with the percentage value printed on the label?

Purchase a variety of commercial antacids. What volume of 1 M hydrochloric acid (approximately the concentration of HCl in your stomach) can be neutral-

---

*A discussion of moles and molarity can be found in most chemistry textbooks.

ized by 1 g of each antacid? Which antacid is the best buy?

ACID RAIN

Much has been written about acid rain. But did you know that rain is *normally* acidic? Carbon dioxide in the air dissolves in raindrops, giving them a pH between 5 and 6. (A pH less than 7 is acidic.)

Using sensitive pH strips, titration, or a pH meter, test samples of rainwater. Does this pH change as a storm progresses? Does the pH of rain vary from season to season? Is geography related to acid rain; that is, does the pH of rain vary with location? Is snow acidic?

ACID-BASE INDICATORS

You may have used litmus paper, pH paper, or indicators such as bromthymol blue or phenolphthalein, but early chemists used natural indicators that can be obtained from fruits and vegetables.

To see an example of this, pour some unsweetened grape juice into a glass. Dilute about 1:9 with water to reduce the color intensity. Add a drop or two of household ammonia to some of the diluted grape juice. What color is grape juice in a base? Now add vinegar until the color of the liquid changes. What color is grape juice in an acid? **Do not drink this or any other solution you make.**

To prepare extracts from the skins of radishes, peaches, tomatoes, rhubarb, red apples, and turnips or from red cabbage, red onions, cherries, beets, or blueberries, chop each material to be tested in a blender. Remove the chopped skin, fruit, or vegetable and place it in a beaker. Cover with distilled water and warm (don't boil) for an hour. Pour off the liquid into another beaker. Dilute with water if necessary.

Add 1 M HCl to the extract you have prepared until the pH falls to 2 as indicated by a pH meter. Slowly add a dilute solution of NaOH drop by drop, recording color and pH as you go.

Would any material or combination of materials that you tried make a universal indicator?

SPEEDY ALKA-SELTZER

Watch what happens when you drop an Alka-seltzer tablet into a glass of water. The bubbles that you see are formed by a gas. You could measure the rate of the reaction by collecting the gas in a graduated cylinder and finding how fast it is produced.

What gas is produced when Alka-seltzer reacts with water? Which ingredients in these tablets are responsible for the gas produced in water?

Design and carry out experiments to see how each of the following factors affects the rate of the reaction: temperature, concentration of reactants, concentration of products, pressure, surface area of reactants. What do you find?

THE THICKNESS
OF ALUMINUM FOIL

Cut a piece of aluminum about 10 cm on a side from a roll of heavy-duty aluminum foil. Cut another piece from a roll of thinner aluminum foil. Weigh both samples to the nearest 0.01 g. Determine the area of both sheets. The density of aluminum is 2.7 g/cm^3. What is the volume of each sheet? Using their volumes and areas, determine the thickness of each sheet.

HOW BIG IS A MOLECULE?

You have probably seen the rainbow-colored film that forms when a thin layer of motor oil floats on a puddle of water. Some substances that are insoluble in, and less dense than, water will spread out into a very thin layer on water. One such substance is oleic acid. If you could determine the thickness of an oleic acid layer on water, you would have an estimate of the maximum size of a molecule of this oily substance. If the layer spreads out until it is one molecule thick, your estimate could be quite close to the actual size of an oleic acid molecule.

To make this estimate, pour water into a large, flat tray, such as the kind found in cafeterias, until the water is about a centimeter deep. When the water is still, sprinkle a fine, powdery layer of chalk dust on its surface. You can do this by rubbing a piece of chalk over sandpaper or by rubbing a finger along a blackboard eraser. Next, bend a fine piece of wire into a narrow V-shape. Wind the upper ends of the wire together and use a clothespin to hold the wire. Dip the V into some alcohol to clean it. When it's dry, dip only the very tip of the V into some oleic acid. Because a normal-size drop would cover a small pond, you want only a tiny drop of the liquid to cling to the wire.

Make a rough estimate of the drop's volume by asking someone to hold the clothespin while you use a magnifier and ruler to estimate the diameter of the drop. By assuming that the drop is either a cube or a sphere, you will be able to estimate its volume later.

Dip the tip of the wire into the center of the water. You will see the oleic acid spread pushing the fine powder outward and leaving a circle that defines the size of the oleic acid layer. Dip the wire tip into the water several times to be sure all the oleic acid has been transferred.

Measure the average diameter of the oleic acid layer.

Calculate the oleic acid's volume and its area on the water. You can then determine the thickness of the layer and, therefore, the maximum height of an oleic acid molecule. What do you find? If you assume the molecules are cube-shaped, how many molecules were in the tiny drop? If these molecules were arranged end to end, how many times would they wrap around the earth?

Find the density of oleic acid. What was the mass of the tiny droplet? What is the mass of an oleic acid molecule on the basis of your data? The actual mass of an oleic acid molecule is 4.7×10^{-22} g. (If you don't understand this terminology—called scientific notation—look in a good science or math textbook.) How close were you? What was the major source of error in this experiment?

To obtain a more accurate value for the volume of oleic acid that was placed on the water, you can dissolve 5 ml of oleic acid in 95 ml of alcohol. Then take 5 ml of this solution and mix it with 45 ml of alcohol. After calibrating an eyedropper so that you know how many drops of oleic acid are in 1 ml, use the dropper to place 1 drop of the dilute oleic acid on a water surface as before. Predict the diameter of the layer when you add a second drop.

What do you find the maximum thickness of a molecule to be this time?

Design an experiment to show that it is oleic acid and not alcohol that accounts for the displacement of the fine powder on the water in this experiment.

ESTIMATING THE MAXIMUM VOLUME OF AN ION

An ion, like an atom or a molecule, is very small. Because some ions are colored, you can dilute the ions over and over again until the color disappears. Why does this method enable you to estimate the volume of an ion?

Dissolve 10 cm^3 of potassium permanganate (KMnO$_4$) in enough water to make 100 ml of solution.

Which ion is the source of the color? What is the approximate volume of $KMnO_4$ in each milliliter of solution? Dilute the sample by adding 1 ml of this solution to 99 ml of water. What volume of $KMnO_4$ is now present in each milliliter of the dilute solution? Continue diluting successive samples until you can see no evidence of the characteristic color through even a deep sample of the solution. What is the maximum volume of permanganate ions according to your results?

OXIDATION AND THE CORROSION OF IRON

Oxidation is defined as the loss of electrons by an atom or ion. Of course, we can't see electrons being transferred from one atom to another, but we do see the effects of oxidation when large numbers of atoms are oxidized. For example, we recognize that iron has been oxidized when we see the rust that results from this process. If iron is oxidized from the metallic state to ferrous ions, we can explain that reaction by the equation below:

$$Fe \longrightarrow Fe^{++} + 2e^-$$

If something loses electrons, something else must gain them. A substance that gains electrons is said to be reduced. For example, when iron rusts or corrodes, the electrons its atoms lose may be gained by either hydrogen ions or oxygen and water molecules as shown by these equations:

$$2H^+ + 2e^- \rightarrow H_2 \text{ or } O_2 + 2H_2O + 4e^- \rightarrow 4OH^-$$

The presence of ferrous ions can be detected with the compound potassium ferricyanide [$K_3Fe(CN)_6$], which reacts with ferrous ions to form the deep-blue precipitate ferrous ferricyanide, $Fe_3[Fe(CN)_6]_2$. If hydroxide ions form, they can be detected by the indicator phe-

nolphthalein, which turns pink in a basic solution. You can use these chemical tests to investigate the corrosion of iron.

Don't forget to wear your safety goggles!

Heat approximately 200 ml of water in a 400-ml beaker. When the water is boiling, add 2 g of agar-agar powder with constant stirring. Once the agar has dissolved, remove the heat and add the following indicators: about 10 drops of 0.10 M potassium ferricyanide and 10 drops of phenolphthalein, which is made by dissolving 1 g of powdered phenolphthalein in 50 ml of water and 50 ml of ethyl alcohol.

While the agar is cooling, place two shiny iron nails that you have cleaned with steel wool in each of two petri dishes. In the first dish, bend one of the nails with a pair of pliers. In the second dish, wrap one nail tightly with a piece of heavy copper wire leaving plenty of space between the wire turns; wrap the other nail with a strip of zinc about 3 mm wide. You can cut the strip from a thin sheet of zinc.

Once the agar is lukewarm but not jelled, pour it into the two dishes so that the nails are completely covered. Allow the agar to harden as you watch for any indication of oxidation and reduction around the nails. Examine the nails periodically and record your observations. What is the effect of *working* the metal? (Note what has happened at the tips, heads, and center of the bent nail.) How does zinc affect the oxidation of iron? How about copper? How do you explain these results?

Try to predict other metals that would prevent the oxidation of an iron nail. Test your predictions experimentally.

It was Galileo and Newton who changed the study of our natural world from philosophical discussions to experimental inquiry. They are the fathers of modern science and the first to find basic patterns in the chaos of motion. It was Galileo who revealed to the world that all falling bodies, if air resistance is negligible, accelerate at the same rate as they fall near the earth's surface. And it was Galileo who made it clear that the vertical and horizontal motions of a projectile, be it cannonball or baseball, are independent of one another. But it was Newton who demonstrated that a falling body is merely one example of the effect of gravitational forces that cause all masses to attract one another. And it was Newton who revealed that the acceleration acquired by an object is proportional to the force acting on the object and inversely proportional to the object's mass.

BUILDING BETTER BALANCES

A balance is one of the most valuable tools in science. Figure 14 shows how to build a simple balance.

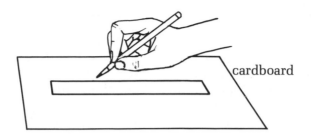

Place a 1–foot ruler on a piece of stiff cardboard. Draw an outline of the ruler with a pencil. Use shears to cut out the rectangle you have outlined.

Draw a line across the exact center of the cardboard. Draw another line 1/4 inch from one side. Use a nail to punch holes at the positions shown here. Number the holes as shown.

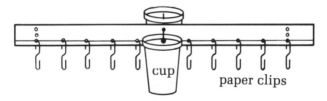

Push the nail through the top center hole. Support the ends of the nail with two large cans, glasses, or books. Unfold 10 paper clips and put them in the holes along the bottom of the cardboard beam. If the beam is not level, trim a little cardboard off the heavy end.

Figure 14   How to make a balance

When you've made the balance, get a dozen or more *identical* steel washers. By hanging various combinations of washers on the beam, see if you can find a rule to help you balance the beam. For example, if someone hangs on the right side of the balance, two washers 3 inches (8 cm) from the center of the beam and three washers 2 inches (5 cm) from the same point, can you use your formula to predict where to hang three washers so that the balance beam will be level?

When you think you've mastered this problem, invite a friend to play a game of "balance." Hang some washers on one side of the balance. Then hand your friend a fixed number of washers and challenge him or her to balance the beam in one move. Then let your friend challenge you.

Do you think the position of the nail (the fulcrum) at the center of the beam has any effect on the balance? To find out, set up the balance as shown in Figure 15. If the beam isn't quite level, add a little clay to the pan on the light side. With the nail through the top center hole, how many drops of water can you add to

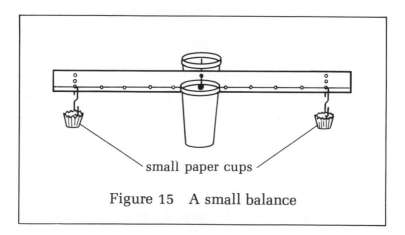

small paper cups

Figure 15   A small balance

one balance pan before it touches the table? Repeat the experiment with the nail through the middle hole and again with the nail through the lower hole.

In which position is the balance most sensitive (most responsive to added weight)?

Does the position from which the pans at the ends of the beam are suspended have any effect on the sensitivity of the balance? How about the distance of the pans from the center of the beam? How about the mass of the object being weighed?

Try to explain why the sensitivity of the balance is affected by the factors you have investigated. Then design and build a sturdier balance that will enable you to weigh objects to at least the nearest hundredth of a gram. Can you build a balance that will weigh light objects to a thousandth of a gram?

AN INCLINED PLANE

Inclined planes are among the simple machines. But how does an inclined plane make work any easier?

To find out, hang a heavy toy truck or laboratory cart from a spring balance. How much does the cart weigh? Place the cart on a board tipped at various angles above a level floor or table as shown in Figure 16. Measure the force, along a direction parallel to the board, that is required to support the truck when the board is tipped at various angles. How is the force required to support the truck related to the angle that the board makes with the floor?

How does the *work* required to lift the truck to a certain height compare with the work required to pull the truck along an incline to the same height? (Work is defined as the product of a force and the distance, parallel to the force, through which that force acts.)

Do inclined planes enable us to do less work, or do they make our work easier?

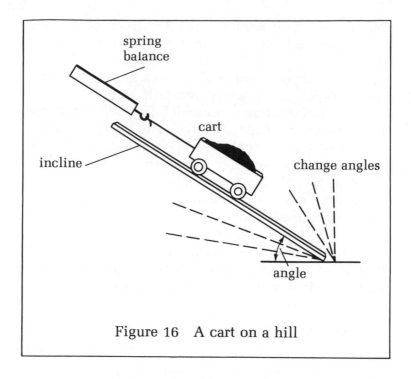

Figure 16   A cart on a hill

THE SLIPPERY SUBJECT
OF FRICTION

The only way you can walk is to push against the earth's surface. When you push back against the ground, the earth pushes forward on your foot. It's the force on your foot that accelerates you forward. If you have ever tried to walk along an icy sidewalk or a highly polished floor, you know it's a difficult task. You can't push as hard as you can when you walk on a rubber mat or a concrete sidewalk. The reason you can't push as hard is because there is very little friction between your feet and the ice or polished floor. Friction is always present when one surface rubs against another. Sometimes the force of friction is large; sometimes it's very small.

With the apparatus shown in Figure 17, you can measure the frictional force when various surfaces rub together. Washers, weights, or a spring balance can be used to measure the force needed to make a block slide across a level surface at constant speed. The force opposing the force you apply to the block is friction. What would happen to the speed of the block if you pulled on it and there were no friction?

Tape different kinds of materials to the block and to the board and record the force needed to move the block for each run you make. Use waxed paper, aluminum foil, newspaper, cardboard, sandpaper, or strips of felt or other cloth. Rubber bands could be put around the block, thumbtacks inserted into the block,

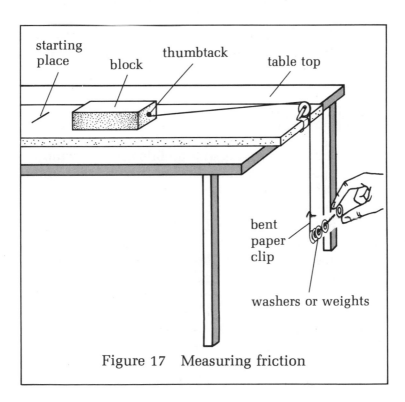

Figure 17   Measuring friction

or round pencils placed under the block. Which combination of surfaces produces the most friction? Which combination gives the least friction?

How does the weight of the block affect friction? If you place a second block on the one you are pulling, does the force required to move the block at constant speed double?

Does the area of contact between the block and the board affect the friction between the surfaces?

Is starting friction (the force needed to get the block moving) greater than kinetic friction (the force needed to keep the block moving at constant speed)?

How could you determine the frictional force by lifting the board and measuring the angle between board and floor when the block slides at a constant speed?

To see what motion is like without friction, you might like to build the frictionless "air car" shown in Figure 18.

ROLLING WHEELS,
SLIDING WHEELS

Watch a slowly moving automobile closely when the driver applies the brakes. Do the front or rear brakes grab first?

Find a toy car with wheels that turn freely. Watch it roll down a smooth incline such as a wide board as you raise the board. Next, use two strong rubber bands to secure both the front and rear wheels so that they cannot turn. (The brakes are locked.) Place the car on the incline again. Does it move more or less easily than before? Why?

Remove the rubber band from the front wheels so that only the rear wheels are locked. Again, place the car on the incline and watch it descend. What happens? Finally, let the car go down the incline with the

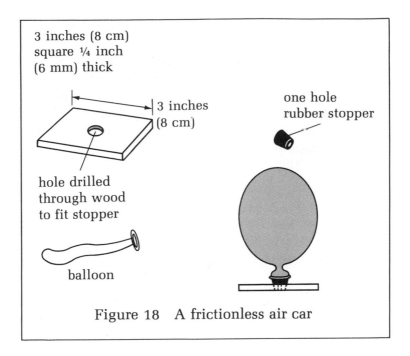

3 inches (8 cm) square ¼ inch (6 mm) thick

3 inches (8 cm)

hole drilled through wood to fit stopper

one hole rubber stopper

balloon

Figure 18   A frictionless air car

front wheels locked and the rear ones free to turn. What happens this time?

How do you explain these differences? What does this experiment have to do with your observation on automobile brakes?

LAUNCHING AND MAPPING PROJECTILES

Drop a ball. It falls because the force of gravity pulls it toward the center of the earth. If you throw a ball, it travels in a curved path because it moves horizontally as it falls. Galileo said that the horizontal and vertical motions were independent. This means that if you throw a ball horizontally and drop another one from the same height, both balls will strike the ground at the same time.

To analyze projectile motion, build a ramp that will launch balls horizontally. Figure 19 shows you how to build this launching ramp from a grooved ruler, a board, several nails, and a block.

Let a marble roll down the ramp. At the moment it leaves the edge of the ruler, drop another marble or ball from exactly the same height. Do both spheres reach the floor at the same time? If they do, you'll hear one "thud" instead of two. Repeat the experiment

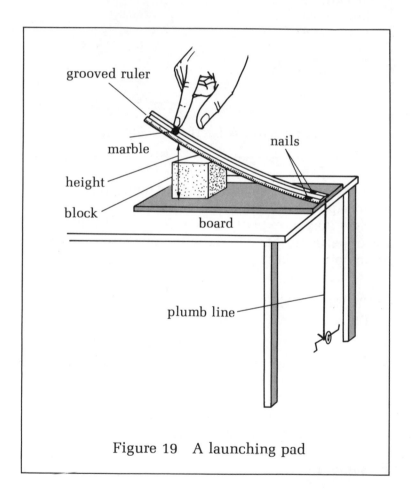

Figure 19   A launching pad

several times. What do you find? Does it matter if the ball you drop is heavier than the marble?

Does the height from which you release the marble on the ramp affect the distance that it travels horizontally?

Let a marble roll down the ramp from different heights. To see how far it travels horizontally before reaching the floor, tape a series of white papers to the floor in the vicinity where the marble lands. Cover the white paper with carbon paper so that the marble will leave a mark when it strikes the paper. Does the height of the marble's release on the ramp affect the distance it travels horizontally? If you double the *vertical* height of release, does the horizontal distance double?

Plot a graph of the horizontal distance traveled by the marble versus the height from which it was released. Can you find a relationship between these two variables?

If the launcher is higher above the floor, will it change the horizontal distance the marble travels before it lands? Does tilting the ramp up or down affect the horizontal distance the marble travels?

By placing the launching ramp near a wall, you can map the path of the projectile. Tape a large sheet of white paper to the wall. Have a friend release the marble from the top of the ramp. Draw a vertical line with a pencil about 3 or 4 inches (8 to 10 cm) from the end of the ramp. Watch the marble as it passes the line. Make a short horizontal line at the point where you think the marble crosses the vertical line. Check it several times by watching the marble as it moves across the lines. Repeat this process at a number of places all along the marble's path.

When you have plenty of points, connect them with a bright colored marking pen or crayon. Watch the marble as it moves from the end of the ramp to the floor. It should follow closely the path you have marked.

What is the shape of the path? What does it tell you about the horizontal and vertical speeds of the marble as it moves? How could you measure these speeds at different times into the marble's flight? Will a larger marble or a steel ball follow the same path?

A BASEBALL PROJECTILE

Galileo showed us that a projectile—a ball, bullet, or other object thrown or shot into the air—will maintain a constant horizontal speed as it accelerates (increases its speed) vertically due to gravity. To see this for yourself, drop a water balloon or a sealed bag of sand as you ride a bicycle over a target marked on a sidewalk. If you drop the bag when it is directly above the target, does it fall on the target? Where should you drop it if it is to hit the target?

You might also drop a tennis ball as you walk along a hallway. Do you have to stop to catch the ball? Or does the ball maintain the horizontal speed it had because it was in your hand? Where do you find the ball if you do stop walking after releasing it?

You can use what Galileo taught us to measure the average force that you exert when you throw a baseball. To throw a baseball, you do work on it and it acquires kinetic energy. Its kinetic energy, KE, is equal to the product of the average force, F, that you exert and the distance, d, through which that force acts. How can you measure the distance, d?

The kinetic energy of the ball is given by:

$$KE = F \times d = \frac{1}{2}mv^2 = \frac{1}{2}m(v_x^2 + v_y^2)$$

In this equation, v_x is the horizontal velocity of the ball, v_y is the vertical velocity of the ball at the moment it is thrown, and m is the mass of the ball.

You can determine the horizontal veloc
ball by measuring the distance it traveled ho
and the time it took to travel that distanc
watch will be helpful in measuring the flig
the ball.

Since the acceleration due to gravity, g, is 9.8
meters per second per second (m/s^2) for all bodies, if
we ignore air resistance, we can find the vertical velocity from the equation:

$$2V_v = gt,$$

where t is the total time the ball is in the air. What do
you find to be the average force that you exerted on
the ball?

Estimate the time it took to throw the ball. To
check up on your estimate, you can calculate the time
to throw the ball from the momentum of the ball at
the moment it was released and the average force that
you exerted:

momentum (mv) = average force (F)
$\times$ time the force was exerted (t)

How close was your estimated time to the time you
calculated?

Throw a ball straight up into the air. From the time
it takes for the ball to return to your hand, you can
calculate the speed of the ball at the moment you
released it.

Have some of your friends hit a pitched ball. For
each fly ball or line drive determine the horizontal
distance the ball travels and its time of flight. From
that data, calculate the velocity of the ball and the
angle that the ball's path makes with the horizontal as
it leaves the bat.

What path angle gives the ball its greatest distance
for any given velocity?

What error is introduced by measuring the distance to the point where the ball strikes the ground?

[79]

EGG DROPS

There's no replacement cost involved in throwing or dropping baseballs; these spheres don't normally break or shatter. But what about eggs?

Design a container into which you can place an egg, drop it from a second or third story onto a concrete sidewalk, and still have an egg that is not cracked or broken.

When you've perfected your container, you might want to enter or sponsor an egg-dropping contest.

BOUNCING BALLS

Have you ever heard that the bounciness of old tennis balls can be restored by heating them? Design an experiment to test this idea. You might also see if temperature has an effect on the bounciness of other balls—baseball, lacrosse, golf, and, of course, Super Ball.

Do different kinds of balls differ significantly in their bounciness? Does the surface on which they bounce have an effect? Why won't a ball bounce to a height greater than the height from which it was dropped? Test your hypothesis.

PENDULUMS AND SPRINGS

Galileo realized that the to-and-fro motion of a pendulum could be used to keep time. But what makes a pendulum run fast or slow? And how can such a clock be adjusted to keep proper time?

Build a pendulum as shown in Figure 20. You can change the mass of the bob by adding more washers to the paper clip. You can change the length of the pendulum, as measured from support point to center of bob, by changing the length of the string. The amplitude of the swing can be changed by pulling the bob

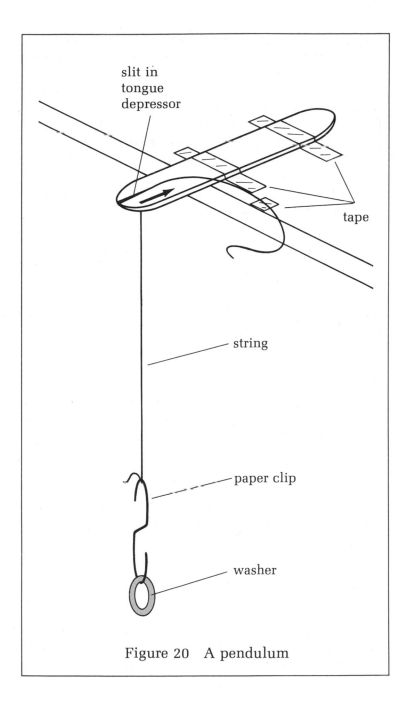

slit in
tongue
depressor

tape

string

paper clip

washer

Figure 20   A pendulum

farther to one side before releasing it. To measure the period of a pendulum—the time for it to make one complete swing, over and back—you can count the number of swings in 30 seconds or 1 minute and then divide the time by the number of swings.

Design experiments to find out how the period of a pendulum is related to the mass of the bob, to the length of the pendulum, and to the amplitude of the swing. What do you find?

Hang a spring, such as a screen-door spring, from a support. Then hang a mass from the bottom of the spring. If you release the mass, you will see that it bounces up and down with a constant period.

Is the period of this oscillating spring, like the period of a pendulum, independent of the mass that is hung on it? How is the period of the spring related to the mass it supports? Do different springs have the same period if they support the same mass?

AN UNDECIDED SPRING

Hang a mass on a spring and watch the mass oscillate up and down. Keep changing the mass until you find a *critical mass*—one that causes the spring to change back and forth between an up-and-down and a back-and-forth (pendulumlike) motion.

After you've watched this "undecided" spring for a while, see if you can develop an explanation for its undecided mode of motion. How can you test your hypothesis?

BUILDING A BETTER KITE OR PAPER AIRPLANE

Many people like to build and fly kites and/or paper airplanes. You might like to try your hand at building the world's best kite or paper airplane. (Or maybe you'll settle for the best in your state or city.) There are contests for people who do this kind of thing. Keep your eye out for such contests as you explore the art and science of kite and paper airplane design and construction.

IS YOUR BICYCLE EFFICIENT?

The efficiency of a machine is defined as the ratio of the energy or work put out by the machine to the work or energy put into it.

Is your bicycle an efficient machine? Design a method for testing the efficiency of your bike. If your bike has gears, does the efficiency depend on which gear the bike is in? Does it depend on the weight of the rider? On tire pressure?

6
HEAT: A FORM
OF ENERGY

If you live in a region where the winters are cold, you will hear people, perhaps your own parents, talking about heating costs. Homes and apartments in the United States and Canada are usually heated by burning oil, coal, wood, or natural gas, or with the heat supplied by electricity or the sun. Of course, electricity often comes from power plants that burn coal, oil, or natural gas, so electric heat is frequently the energy supplied by fossil fuels, once removed. In all these cases, energy in one form, be it the chemical energy stored in fossil fuels, the radiant energy in sunlight, or electrical energy, is changed into thermal energy, or heat.

The cost of heating your home depends on many factors: the size of the house, how cold it is outside, how warm it is inside, how long it must be heated, and how well it is insulated.

Humankind has made use of heat throughout history, but it was only 200 years ago that scientists such as Joseph Black and Benjamin Thompson began to investigate heat in an effort to understand what it was and how it behaved.

CAUTION: Many of the projects in this chapter MUST be conducted under supervision of your science teacher or of another knowledgeable adult. Check with your teacher before beginning any project. He or she will tell you whether the project is safe to do alone. **Always wear safety goggles and handle hot objects and liquids carefully. Work in clean, orderly space to minimize fire hazard.**

THE HEAT TO MELT ICE

Joseph Black, a Scottish chemist, lived in the eighteenth century, a period when scientists were struggling to understand the nature of heat. Black observed that ice and snow melt very slowly with no change in temperature. Yet, when snow melted in his bare hands, he could feel huge amounts of heat flowing out of his hands. Black set out to find how much heat was required to melt a fixed amount of ice. You can perform an experiment similar to his and use similar reasoning to answer his question.

Black compared the heat needed to melt ice with the heat required to warm an equal weight of water through 8°F (4.5°C). He poured equal amounts of water into two containers. He froze the water in one container; the water in the second container he cooled to the freezing point (32°F or 0°C). He then placed both containers, one with ice at 32°F (0°C), the other with water at the same temperature, in a large room where the temperature remained at 47°F (8°C) throughout the experiment. After half an hour, the temperature of the water had risen to 40°F (4°C). Ten hours passed before the same mass of ice melted and reached the same temperature. Try a similar experiment of your own. Do you get similar results?

Black reasoned that the same amount of heat would enter both the water and ice at the same time. They were in the same room and had about the same amount of area exposed to the warmer air. In view of the relative times to bring both samples to 40°F (4°C), Black argued that it required twenty times as much heat to melt ice as it did to raise the temperature of water through 8°F (4.5°C). Do you agree with Black's reasoning?

It takes 1 calorie to raise the temperature of 1 g of water 1°C. One BTU (British thermal unit) is the heat required to raise the temperature of 1 pound of water 1°F. How much heat, in calories, is required to melt 1 g of ice? How many BTUs of heat are required to melt 1 pound of ice?

Design an experiment of your own to find the heat needed to melt a fixed weight of ice.

Why did Black measure the time for the water to reach 40°F (4°C) rather than 47°F (8°C), which was the temperature of the room? To help answer this question, you might try plotting a graph of the temperature of ice water as it warms up to room temperature versus time. How is the flow of heat from one substance to another related to the temperature difference between them?

Design an experiment to measure the heat required to boil away a gram or a pound of water. How do you think Joseph Black would have done this?

CALORIC MASS

Joseph Black did not attempt to explain what heat was. He was content to learn, through experimentation, how it behaved. Other scientists theorized that heat was an invisible fluid, which they called *caloric*. They thought that caloric flowed from warm bodies, which were warm because they possessed abundant caloric, to cooler bodies that had less caloric.

Benjamin Thompson (Count Rumford), thinking about the caloric theory and Black's experiments that revealed the large amounts of heat required to melt ice, suggested that if heat really is an invisible fluid, ice should weigh less than the water from which it is formed.

Explain Thompson's argument. Then design an experiment to test Thompson's reasoning based on the caloric theory. What do you find?

If you would like to know how Thompson investigated this idea, read *Count Rumford, Physicist Extraordinary* by Sanborn C. Brown (Anchor Books, 1962).

HOW HOT IS A FLAME?

If you try to measure the temperature of a flame by putting a thermometer into it, you will succeed only in breaking the thermometer. You need a less direct method for finding the temperature of something as hot as a flame.

One approach is to heat a piece of metal in a flame until it has the same temperature as the flame. Then add the metal to some water and record the temperature change. (Temperature changes are often written as ΔT. The symbol Δ is the Greek letter delta. It is often used in mathematics and science to mean "change in." The temperature difference between two temperature readings T_2 and T_1 can be expressed as $T_2 - T_1$ or as ΔT.) If you know the mass of the water and its temperature change, you can determine the amount of heat transferred from the metal to the water. Since the heat gained by the water was lost by the metal, these two heats can be set equal to each other. From the specific heat of the metal, which you can find from a table if you know what kind of metal you used, you can write:

Heat lost by metal = heat gained by water
Mass of metal × specific heat × ΔT (metal)
= mass of water × ΔT (water)
Mass of metal × specific heat × $(T_{flame} - T_{final})$
= mass of water × $(T_{final} - T_{initial})$

The only thing you don't know in this equation is the temperature of the flame, which you can easily calculate.

To do the experiment you will need, in addition to the flame, a small piece of metal, one that will fit in the flame (a small steel washer is fine), an insulated cup, cold water, something to hold the washer in the flame, and a thermometer, preferably one that will measure to the nearest 0.1°C. **Wear safety goggles and be careful with flames and hot objects.**

Determine the mass of the piece of metal. Then hold the metal in the flame for a period of several minutes. You can use an unfolded paper clip, held by a clamp-type clothespin outside the flame, to support the metal.

Once the metal is hot, have a friend place a small volume of cold water in an insulated cup and measure the water's temperature. Remove the thermometer and quickly (so as not to lose heat to the air) transfer the metal to the cold water. Stir the water and record the final temperature.

Repeat the experiment several times. How can you decide how long to heat the metal? How much water should you use?

What is the temperature of the flame?

Use this technique to determine the temperatures of a variety of flames. You might test the flames of alcohol burners, bunsen burners, candles, gas stoves, and matches. Which flame is hottest?

HEAT LOSS AND
SURFACE AREA

Heating costs depend to some extent on the size of your house. But heat can escape only through the surface of a house, so you might guess that heat losses are related to the surface area of your home.

To test this idea, make two pieces of ice that have the *same* volume but different surface areas. Because the ice cakes are made with the same mass of water, it will take the same amount of heat to melt each of them. To melt 1 g of ice requires 80 calories, 334 joules, or 0.31 BTUs. How much heat is required to melt each piece of ice that you made?

Once the ice cakes are thoroughly frozen, fill a bucket or large container with water. You should use a lot of water to melt the ice so that its temperature doesn't change significantly; after all, the temperature difference between the ice and the water could affect the melting rate. After measuring the dimensions of the ice cakes so that you can calculate their surface areas, add the ice to the water. Stir the water constantly so that the surfaces of both pieces of ice will be in contact with the water and not their own meltwater. After 10 seconds remove both pieces of ice and quickly dry and weigh them.

How long does it take each piece of ice to melt? How much heat flowed into one of the ice cakes per second? How much heat flowed into the other piece of ice per second? What was the surface area of each piece of ice?

Compare the two ratios:

A. $$\frac{\text{Heat flow into ice cake \#1 in one second}}{\text{Heat flow into ice cake \#2 in one second}}$$

B. $$\frac{\text{Area of ice cake \#1}}{\text{Area of ice cake \#2}}$$

What do you find? What does it tell you about the rate of heat flow and surface area? Why didn't you simply wait until all the ice had melted and then calculate the heat flow per second? How will the heating costs of a house with a large surface area compare with one with a small surface area if all other factors are the same?

HEAT LOSS AND
TEMPERATURE DIFFERENCE

From experience, you know that the rate at which heat flows from your body depends on the temperature of the air or water around you. If you step outside on a cold day, you'll soon begin to shiver unless you are wearing warm clothing. Shivering makes your muscles work, producing more heat in your body. On a hot day, you sweat and heat is absorbed from your body to vaporize the perspiration.

To see how the temperature difference between two substances affects heat flow, add 100 ml of hot water to each of two cups. The temperature of the water in the two cups should be the same. Leave one cup in a warm room; put the other one in a cold place such as a refrigerator or in a protected place outdoors if it is cold weather. Record the temperature of the water in each container at 1-minute intervals. At some point in your investigation record the air temperature around each container.

To see how the cooling rates compare, plot a graph of temperature on the vertical axis versus time on the horizontal axis. Plot both sets of data on the same set of axes. How does the temperature difference between the water and air affect the rate of heat loss?

Using either of the curves you plotted, you can determine the slope of the graph at a series of points. From these slopes, the temperatures, and the mass of the water, plot a graph of the rate of heat loss versus the difference in temperature between the water and its surroundings.

What does this graph tell you?

Design an experiment, using identical ice cubes and large volumes of warm and cold water, to see how the ratio of the melting rates in the warm and cold water compares with the ratio of the temperature difference between the ice and the water in which the ice melts. Since the melting rate is proportional to the rate at which heat flows into the ice, you are really comparing the rate of heat flow with the temperature difference between ice and the heat source. What do your results reveal?

INSULATION AND R VALUES

Heat losses or heat flow, as you have seen from experiments above, are proportional to surface area and the temperature difference between warm and cold substances. Heat losses are also related to time; if the temperature difference and surface area between two substances remain constant, twice as much heat will flow in twice the time. There is one other factor in measuring heat losses: the conductivity of the material that lies between the warm and cold substances. Thus heat loss can be calculated from the equation:

$$\text{Heat loss} = \text{conductivity} \times \text{area} \times \text{time} \times (T_{inside} - T_{outside})$$

Heating engineers measure conductivity in units of BTUs/hour/square foot/degree Fahrenheit (BTU/h/ ft^2/F°). Suppose a warm air space surrounded by 10 square feet of 3/4-inch fiberboard loses 50 BTUs of heat per hour when the temperature of the warm air is 10 degrees higher than the cooler surrounding air. The conductivity, U, of the fiberboard would be

$$U = 50 \text{ BTU}/1 \text{ h}/10 \text{ ft}^2/10F° = 0.5 \text{ BTU}/h/ft^2/F°$$

Homeowners want insulating materials that do not conduct heat well; consequently, insulating materials are rated according to their resistance to conduct heat. A material's ability to resist heat flow is measured in terms of its R value, which is just the inverse of conductivity:

$$R = 1/U$$

The conductivity of the fiberboard above was 0.5 BTU/h/ft²/F°. Its R value would be

$$R = 1/U = 1/0.5 = 2 \text{ ft}^2\text{-h-F°/BTU}$$

The conductivity is turned upside down so that the numbers consumers have to deal with are greater than 1. A material with a large R value is a good insulator.

Here's a way to measure the R value of cardboard. Put a 100-watt light bulb in a good-size, sealed, cardboard box that rests on a couple of small blocks so that the entire surface of the box is exposed to the cooler air around it. Place the bulb of a thermometer through the box about halfway up one side so you can measure the average temperature inside the box. Another thermometer can be used to measure the air temperature outside the box.

When the temperature inside the box becomes constant, we can assume that heat losses from the box equal the rate at which heat is being generated by the bulb inside. We know the heat generated is 100 joules per second because it is a 100-watt bulb and, if the box is well sealed so that light does not escape, any energy that appears as light will be transformed to thermal energy when absorbed by the materials within. Using this information, the area of the box, the temperatures inside and outside the box, and the time—1 second—determine the R value of the cardboard.

Now that you know the R value of a certain thickness of cardboard, you can determine the R values of other materials by comparing the rate at which they lose heat with that of an equal area of cardboard. What is the R value of the Styrofoam in coffee cups? What about the R values of other insulating materials such as fiber glass, rock wool, cellulose, vermiculite, newspapers, glass, and wood? How is the R value related to the thickness of a material?

How do your R values compare with those found in tables in books on home energy or at a lumber store?

What are degree days? Using what you know about heat losses and degree days, calculate the heat losses from your home or school over a 1 year period. Translate that into the money needed to buy fuel to supply the heat. How could heat losses and, therefore, heating costs be reduced in your home or school?

HEATING WITH COLORED SOLAR ENERGY

You know that the energy in sunlight can be converted into heat. You probably know also that the white light of sunlight can be broken up into all the colors of the rainbow. But does the color of the light that falls on a solar collector have any effect on the amount of heat produced? Design an experiment to answer that question.

A MODEL SOLAR HOME OR WATER HEATER

Some homes are heated entirely, or partially, by energy from the sun. In a large number of homes, domestic hot water is provided by solar energy.

Design and build a model solar home and/or a model solar collector for heating hot water.

7

ELECTRICITY

In 1791 Luigi Galvani found that connecting two different metals could make a frog's muscle contract just as surely as the spark created by a Leyden jar, an apparatus that stores electricity. About ten years later, Alessandro Volta found that the electricity produced was the result of the two different metals and had nothing to do with the frog. A pile of metal disks arranged in a zinc, copper, zinc, copper fashion with cardboard disks moistened in saltwater between the metals resulted in a continuous flow of electricity when the top and bottom of the pile were connected with a wire. Volta had invented the first electric battery.

In 1831 Michael Faraday showed that electricity can be produced by changing the magnetic field through a coil of wire. This is the principle used to produce electricity in modern power plants. A large coil of wire turns in a magnetic field. The work required to turn the wire is supplied by moving water or by steam that comes from heating water with burning coal, oil, or gas, or from heat supplied by a nuclear reactor. Unlike a battery, in which chemicals that supply the electricity are eventually used up, an electric generator will continue to produce electricity as long as the coil turns in the magnetic field.

BENDING WATER
WITH ELECTRICITY

On a day when the humidity is low, rub a hard rubber rod or a plastic comb or ruler on some woolen clothing. This will give the rod a negative charge. Then bring the rod near a thin stream of water flowing from a faucet. You will see the water bend toward the rod.

What kinds of objects, when rubbed with wool, will produce this effect? Glass rods? Balloons? Other things?

Can you get a similar effect if you rub with cloth other than wool? How about paper?

If you change the sign of the charge by using a glass rod instead of rubber, will the water be repelled by, instead of attracted to, the rod?

[95]

Bending water with electricity

Will other liquid streams show a similar effect when near an electrically charged rod? **Avoid using flammable liquids such as alcohol. A highly charged rod might cause a spark that could ignite the liquid.**

TESTING CONDUCTORS AND NONCONDUCTORS

Solids and liquids through which electricity flows easily are called conductors; materials that do not allow electricity to flow through them are called nonconductors.

You can test different solids and liquids to see if they conduct electricity by placing them in series with a flashlight bulb. Set up the circuit shown in Figure 21. Connect the leads between the battery and the bulb to the ends of a solid you want to test. Test a variety of things: silverware, nails, plastic, pencils and pencil lead, wood, paper, wax, and so on. If the bulb

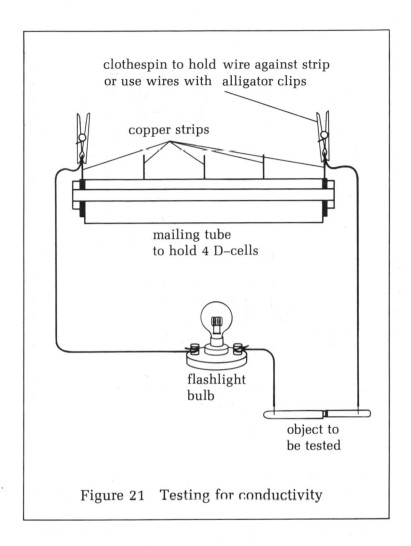

clothespin to hold wire against strip
or use wires with alligator clips

copper strips

mailing tube
to hold 4 D–cells

flashlight
bulb

object to
be tested

Figure 21   Testing for conductivity

lights, the solid is a conductor. Which solids are conductors? What do you know about the solid in the circuit if the bulb doesn't light?

To test the conductivity of liquids, slide two paper
clips over the edge of a medicine cup filled with the
liquid you want to test as shown in Figure 22. At least

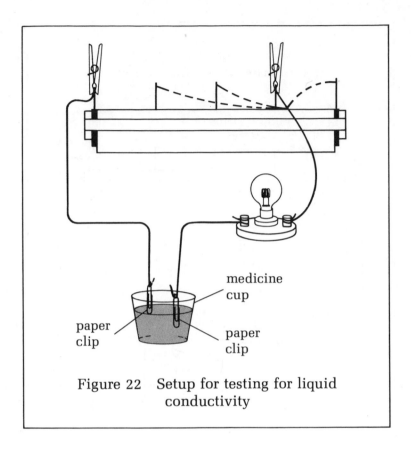

medicine
cup

paper
clip

paper
clip

Figure 22   Setup for testing for liquid
conductivity

the lower half of both paper clips should be in the liquid. Connect the two leads to the paper clip and see if the bulb lights.

You could test such liquids as water, milk, lemon juice, saturated solutions of salt, sugar, and baking soda. Which liquids are conductors?

Repeat your tests for the liquids that appear to be nonconductors. In some of these liquids you may find gas bubbling up around the paper clips even though the bulb doesn't light. What does this suggest? What further tests might you perform?

What are semiconductors?

ELECTRICITY FROM
FRUIT AND NAILS

Volta used two different metals and a salt solution to produce electricity. The electrical cells (D cells, C cells, etc.) that you buy today also consist of two metals immersed in an electrolyte (something that will conduct electricity). You can make some simple electric cells using two metals and a variety of fruits and vegetables as electrolytes.

Gather a number of different fruits and vegetables such as a lemon, an apple, an orange, a potato, a pickle, and a couple of olives. You will also need a sensitive galvanometer or microammeter, wire leads, paper towels, water, and nails or strips made from several different metals such as copper, aluminum, iron, zinc, and nickel.

Shine the metals with steel wool. Clean them this way each time they are used.

Connect one end of each of two wire leads to two different metals (nails or strips). Connect the other ends of the wire leads to the two poles (+ and −) of the meter. Then put the nails into one of the fruits or vegetables. Do you have any evidence that electricity is produced? Can you get the meter needle to move backward (left instead of right)? If the needle does move to the right, what happens if you switch the metals so that their leads to the meter are reversed? Does the electric current measured on the meter depend on how far apart the nails are? Does it depend on how deeply the nails are pushed into the fruit? Does it depend on which nails are used? Does it depend on which fruit or vegetable is used?

Can you get a current to flow if you squeeze two different metals in your fingers? If you touch the metals to your skin? Are you a conductor of electricity?

Which fruit seems to be the best electrolyte?

As you have seen, to make the meter needle move to the right a particular metal of a pair must be connected to the + lead of the meter. Sometimes, in order to make the needle move right, the metal that was connected to the + lead must be connected to the − lead when paired with a different metal. With that in mind, try to establish which of the metals you have is the most *positive* metal. Which is the most *negative* metal?

BUILD A BETTER BATTERY

Now that you have built some simple batteries, read some books and articles about batteries. On the basis of your research, build your own Daniell cell. Build a model lead storage cell. What are the advantages of a lead storage cell over a Daniell cell?

The success of the electric car depends on the development of a battery that can be recharged thousands of times. See if you can make such a battery.

RESISTING ELECTRICITY

The electrical resistance of a circuit element—a bulb, wire, motor, or whatever—is defined as the ratio of the potential difference (voltmeter reading) across the element to the current through the element for a given temperature. With a circuit like the one in Figure 23, you can measure the resistance of any circuit element. Note that the voltmeter is wired in parallel (side-by-side branches) with the element, while the ammeter is in series (one after the other). The battery consists of eight D cells in series.

Measure the resistance of some small resistors. To be sure they don't burn out, and to maintain a nearly constant temperature, place the resistors in a small amount of water. Measure the current and voltage as

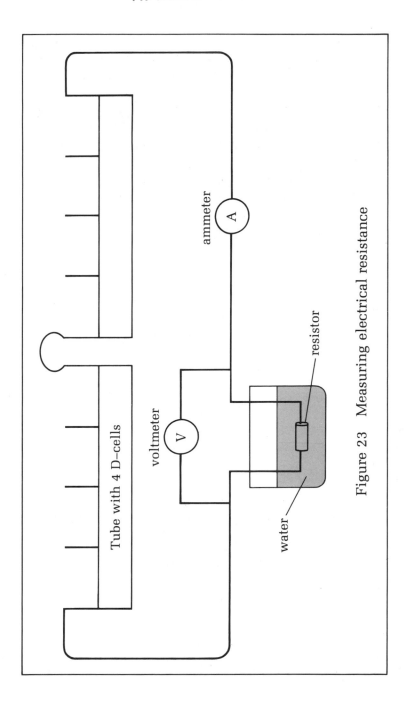

Figure 23   Measuring electrical resistance

you increase the size of your battery from one cell to eight. Plot a graph of voltage versus current. Is the ratio constant? How can you tell? You can also measure the resistance of a number of other circuit elements—small DC electric motors, flashlight bulbs, and various long pieces of wire such as the wires used to replace the heating elements in electric stoves.

How is the resistance of a wire related to its length? How does the resistance of the wire filament in a flashlight bulb change as the wire gets hotter?

What determines the electrical resistance of an electroplating cell such as the one shown in Figure 24?

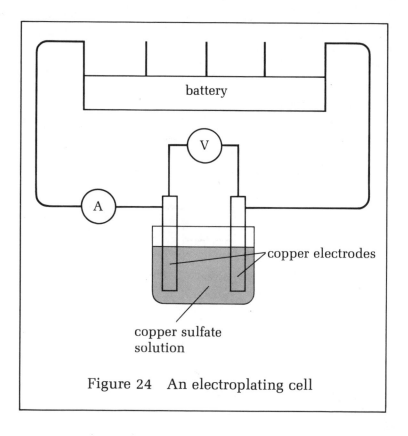

Figure 24   An electroplating cell

What is the resistance of your voltmeter? Of your ammeter? Of a D cell? Of a vacuum tube?

Measure the resistance of each of two resistors. Connect them in series; then connect them in parallel. What happens to the total resistance of the resistors when they are wired in series? when they are wired in parallel?

How do you think the resistance of a wire is related to its cross-sectional area? Find a way to test your prediction. Were you right?

A POSSIBLE SURPRISE

With a flashlight bulb, a socket, a D cell, and some wire leads, you can make a simple circuit that contains a glowing bulb. What do you think will happen if you lower the bulb into a glass of water? Try it. Were you surprised? How can you explain the result? If you have difficulty, think about the electrical resistance of water as compared with metal wires.

Can you predict the result if you repeat the experiment using saltwater in place of plain water?

ENERGY AND
ELECTRIC CHARGE

Does the energy supplied by a flow of charge depend on the quantity of charge?

To find out, you can heat some water in a calorimeter by letting a known amount of electric charge flow through a wire immersed in water. The heating wire can be a short piece of a heating element coil used to repair electric stoves, or you can use a piece of nichrome wire. In either case the wire should have a resistance of about 2 ohms. Since electric current is the rate of charge flow, the total charge that flows is equal to current times time:

Charge (measured in ampere-seconds)
= current (amperes) × time (seconds)

After recording the initial temperature with a thermometer that can read temperature to the nearest 0.1°C, let a current of 4 amps flow through the wire immersed in 100 g of water as shown in Figure 25 (use

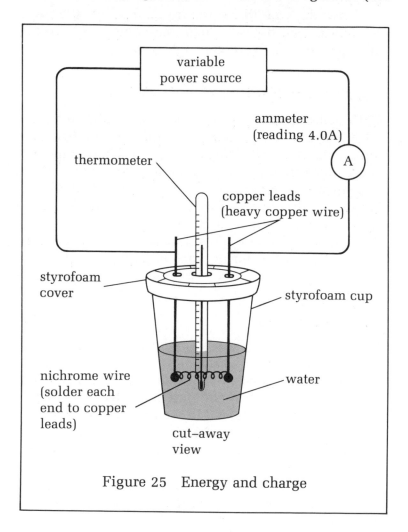

Figure 25   Energy and charge

a low-voltage variable power supply). After 30 seconds, turn off the current, gently stir the water to be sure the heat is evenly distributed, and record the maximum temperature.

Repeat the experiment using another 100 g of *cool* water. This time let the 4-amp current run for 60 seconds. Make two more runs for 90- and 120-second intervals. Why should you start each run with cool water?

What is the relationship between the heat delivered and the quantity of charge?

What is the relationship between the heat per charge and the charge in this experiment in which a constant current flows for different periods of time?

How could you reduce the errors in this experiment?

THE DIRECTION
OF CHARGE FLOW

Using your knowledge of electricity, design experiments to show that electric charge flows in only one direction along wires but in two directions within electric cells and electrolytic solutions.

WHAT DOES A
VOLTMETER MEASURE?

A voltmeter measures *voltage*, or better, *potential difference*. But what does that mean? Here's a way to find out.

Connect a voltmeter to the apparatus shown in Figure 25 (see Figure 26). After recording the temperature of 100 g of water to the nearest 0.1°C, allow a current of 4 amps to flow for 60 seconds. Record the voltmeter reading, current, time, and change in tem-

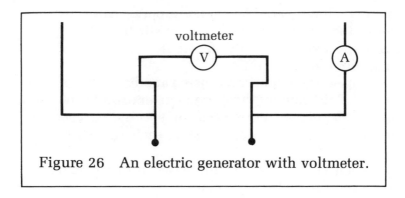

Figure 26   An electric generator with voltmeter.

perature. Since you know that less charge will reduce the heat delivered, you should increase the time as you reduce the current and voltage in succeeding runs. Therefore, in the next run let a current of 3 amps flow for 120 seconds, then 2 amps for 3 minutes, and, finally, 1 amp for 4 minutes.

Calculate the heat delivered in calories and the charge in ampere-seconds for each run. Then plot a graph of *heat per charge* on the vertical axis versus voltage across the heater. What do you find? What does a voltmeter measure?

Write an equation relating heat, current, time, and voltage.

The product voltage $\times$ current $\times$ time is measured in joules. If you measure heat in joules, write an equation relating heat, current, time, and voltage. How many joules are equivalent to 1 calorie?

GENERATING ELECTRICITY

Faraday found that he could generate electricity by changing the magnetic field within a coil of wire. You can duplicate Faraday's feat by moving a bar magnet in and out of a coil of wire connected to a microammeter or galvanometer as shown in Figure 27.

The amount of electricity generated in this simple demonstration is small, and you would quickly tire of moving the magnet. See if you can build a generator that will (1) generate enough electricity to light a flashlight bulb and (2) run continuously without the use of "muscle power."

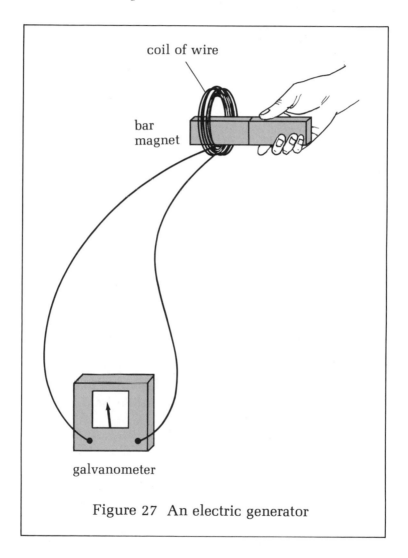

Figure 27 An electric generator

8
BODY-AND-MIND
SCIENCE

Human physiology is the study of the life processes that go on within our bodies. Psychology is the science of mental processes, the activities that go on within our brain. Most people enjoy these subject areas because they're really studying themselves.

CAUTION
• **This chapter includes experiments that should be performed only on people who are healthy and in normal physical condition.**
• If you are thinking of using one of these projects in a science fair, check the rules to make sure that projects involving human beings are allowed.

HOW TIME FLIES

Can you tell when a minute has passed without a watch? How about 5 minutes? An hour? Does time seem to slow down when you are bored and speed up when you are busy? Does time seem to pass faster as you get older?

How good are you at estimating time? When the second hand of a clock reaches 12, turn away from the clock. Don't try to count seconds, but when you think a minute has passed, look at the clock again. Was your guess a short minute or a long one?

Now, try to guess when 5 minutes have passed; when 10 have passed. Try to estimate half an hour. Are you less accurate at estimating long periods than shorter ones?

Try estimating how much time has passed while you read different things such as a novel or a page in a dictionary. Does the kind of material you are reading affect the way you estimate time? Estimate time as you listen to different types of music. Does fast music make time seem to pass faster than slow music? Finally, try to estimate time while you are physically active such as running, cycling, or doing household chores.

Once you've studied your own ability to estimate time and how it is affected by various factors, try the same experiments on a number of other people. Try to find subjects of both sexes and of various ages. Work with each person individually and keep a record of his or her estimates. Record whether their guesses are too long or too short by writing the error as, for example, +12 seconds or −8 seconds. Also record the individual's name, age, and sex and date of the experiment.

Do older people tend to overestimate time has passed? Do females estimate time better than males? Does season affect estimates? What patterns do you find?

LOOKS CAN BE DECEIVING

Look at the optical illusions in Figure 28. A study of these few illusions should convince you that things

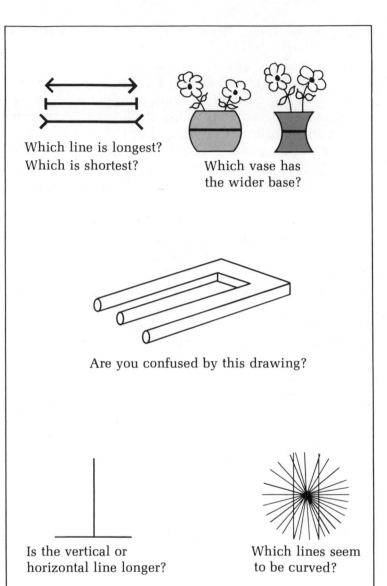

Which line is longest?
Which is shortest?

Which vase has
the wider base?

Are you confused by this drawing?

Is the vertical or
horizontal line longer?

Which lines seem
to be curved?

Figure 28   Optical illusions

are not always the way they appear to be. Things we see can often deceive our brain. Look at the moon as it rises. How does its apparent size compare with its size after it has ascended a few degrees in the sky?

Photograph the moon as it rises and ascends into the sky. Is it really larger on the horizon? Look at the rising moon with your chin on your chest so that you view it through the upper part of your visual field. Does this change its apparent size? Try to explain this lunar illusion.

Design some illusions of your own. Test them on other people and see if you can explain why they create the effects they do.

TO SLEEP
PERCHANCE TO DREAM

Do you move in your sleep? Do you dream? It is likely that we all dream, but many of us don't remember our dreams. Next time you go to sleep, try to remember the last position you were in before you dozed off. Are you in the same position when you wake up? Watch your friends or family members (with their permission, of course) as they sleep. Do they move? Do they talk? Do their eyes move?

You can detect a person's eye movements even if their eyes are closed. Rapid back-and-forth eye movement during sleep is called REM sleep. REM stands for "rapid eye movement." It is during REM sleep that most people dream. If you can watch someone who claims not to dream, you will find that they go through periods of REM sleep about four to six times each night. If you wake that person during REM sleep, they will probably recall what they were dreaming.

If you are a person who doesn't remember dreams, set your alarm clock so that you are awakened half an hour earlier than usual for several mornings. There is a good chance that you will be in REM sleep and hence dreaming. Most people pass through REM sleep shortly before they wake.

You may also be able to remember dreams if, when you first awaken, you think about the first thing that comes to mind. Chances are it may have something to do with the last dream you had before waking, and this will lead you to remember the entire dream.

Keep a record of your dreams. Do you dream about the things you think about or do during the day? Do you often have the same or similar dreams? If awakened, can you go back to sleep and finish a dream? Do you ever solve problems while asleep? Many people do.

What evidence do you have that animals dream? Do dogs and cats have REM sleep?

ARE YOU IN SHAPE?

Here's a way to determine if someone is in good physical condition. It's called the Harvard step test. Simply have the subject step up onto and down from a bench or step thirty times per minute for 4 minutes. The height of the bench should be related to the height of the individual as shown in the chart below.

Height of Step (inches)	Height of Subject (feet, inches)
12	5', 0'' or less
14	5', 0''–5', 3''
16	5', 3''–5', 9''
18	5', 9''–6', 0''
20	6' 0'' or greater

After the subject has completed the test, wait one minute. Then count his or her heartbeats for 30 seconds. Again, count the number of heartbeats in 30 seconds 2 minutes after the exercise and 3 minutes after the exercise.

From the data collected, calculate the recovery index (RI) according to the formula below.

$$RI = \frac{\text{Duration of exercise in seconds} \times 100}{\text{Sum of heartbeats} \times 2}$$

Suppose you collect the following data on a subject:

Time after exercise (minutes)	Number of heartbeats
1–1.5	50
2–2.5	45
3–3.5	40

The RI would be calculated as follows:

$$RI = \frac{240 \times 100}{(50+45+40) \times 2} = \frac{24{,}000}{135 \times 2}$$

$$= \frac{24{,}000}{270} = 89$$

The relationship between one's physical condition and the recovery index is shown below.

Physical condition	Recovery Index
poor	50 or less
fair	50–65
good	65–80
excellent	greater than 80

Test a number of subjects. Are athletes in better shape than nonathletes? Are distance runners in better condition that other athletes? Can you detect those who smoke?

See if you can devise a better test for physical condition. You might include breathing rate as well as heart rate, and you might find the time required for the subject to return to the same heart and breathing rates that existed before the exercise. Maybe your school's coaches would be interested in using your test.

REACTION TIME

Here's a safe bet. Tell your friend she can keep a dollar bill if she can catch it before it falls through her fingers after you release it. A paper dollar is about 6 inches (15 cm) long. If your friend holds her fingers 2 inches (5 cm) from the bottom of the bill, she must react before the dollar falls 4 inches (10 cm), that is, within 0.15 second. Few people have such a fast reaction time.

To measure someone's reaction time, have that person place her fingers around the very bottom of a smooth yardstick that you hold in a vertical position. Tell the subject she is to catch the yardstick between her fingers as soon as possible after she sees it begin to fall. The person should not try to anticipate when you are going to release the yardstick. The chart below allows you to determine the person's reaction time. Can you make a similar chart for reaction time in terms of centimeters that a *meter* stick falls before being caught?

Distance yardstick falls before it is caught (inches)	Reaction time (second)
6	0.18
12	0.25
18	0.31
24	0.35
30	0.40
36	0.43

Test a number of people. Do you find any patterns? Do girls react faster than boys of the same age. Does reaction time change with age? Are athletes faster than nonathletes? Are people whose work requires exceptional manual dexterity, such as surgeons or artists, faster than others? What else do you find?

How were the reaction times in the chart established?

Try to invent a better method for measuring reaction time.

HOW POWERFUL
ARE YOU?

Can you work like a horse? You may be surprised to find that you can.

If you walk up a flight of stairs, you do some work on yourself. If you run up the stairs, you do the same amount of work but in a shorter time. The rate at which work is done is called *power*.

$$\text{Power} = \text{work}/\text{time}$$

Power can be measured in foot•pounds per second, joules per second (watts), or any units of force times distance (work) divided by time. A common unit of power that you've probably heard of is *horsepower*. One horsepower is 550 foot•pounds of work per second, or 746 watts.

To determine how much power you can develop, have someone measure the time it takes you to run up a long flight of stairs. To calculate your power you need to know the *vertical* height of the stairs, your weight, and the time it took you to ascend the stairs. The product of your weight and the height of the stairs is the work you did on yourself. If you divide that work done by the time to do it, you will find your power. For example, if you weigh 120 pounds and run up a flight of stairs 12 feet high in 4 seconds, your power can be calculated as shown below:

$$\text{Power} = \frac{\text{weight} \times \text{height of stairs}}{\text{time}}$$

$$= \frac{120 \text{ lb} \times 12 \text{ ft}}{4 \text{ sec}} = 360 \text{ ft·lb/sec}$$

$$= 0.66 \text{ hp}$$

Try it! How powerful are you?

Use the same method to find how much horsepower other people can develop. What do you find? Is the power that a person can develop related to age? gender? height? weight?

Suppose you measure the power developed over a greater height, say, five flights of stairs instead of one or two. How does this affect an individual's ability to develop power? Can you explain why?

MUSCLE PAIRS

Muscles can do work only when contracting. That's why most muscles come in pairs. Your biceps enable you to bend your forearm toward your shoulder; your triceps are used to straighten or extend your arm. Usually one muscle of a pair is stronger than the other. That is why you can kick harder in a forward direction than in a backward direction.

You can use a bathroom scale to measure the strength of some muscle pairs. Sit on a chair and push your foot forward against a scale that is resting against a wall as shown in Figure 29. How hard can you push forward? Now stand the scale on end against one leg of the chair in which you are seated. Use the other member of the muscle pair to press your heel against the scale. How hard can your muscles push backward?

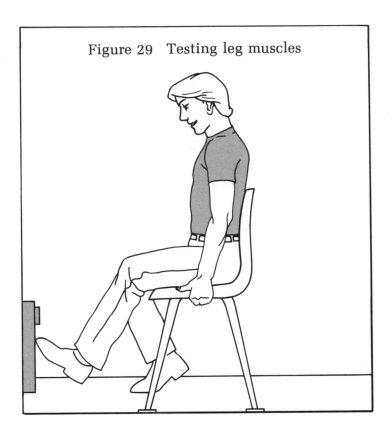

Figure 29   Testing leg muscles

Use the same scale or a spring scale to measure the relative strength of other muscles that are paired. You may want a helper to hold the scale or read it. Look for muscle pairs that move parts of your body in opposite directions. You've already heard of the muscles that flex and extend the lower arm. Similarly, there are muscle pairs that push fingers apart or squeeze them together; muscles that push your toes down or lift them up; muscles that allow you to move your head forward or back. What other muscle pairs can you find? Is one member of a muscle pair always much stronger than the other? Can you increase the strength of the weaker member of a pair through exercise, or will the ratio of the relative strengths of the pair remain constant? What is your strongest muscle?

Compare your muscle strengths with those of other people. Do any have muscle pairs in which the muscle strength of a pair is the opposite of yours? Is the relative strength of paired muscles related to the work or exercise that people do?

MUSCLE FATIGUE

You know that muscles tire through use. To see how much strength your finger muscles lose through use, hold a bathroom scale with one hand on either side. Squeeze as hard as you can. With what force can you squeeze the scale? Put the scale down and open and close your fingers as fast as you can for one minute. Then immediately squeeze the scale again. Have you gained or lost strength in your fingers? How much? How long does it take before your strength is the same as before?

Do the muscles of people stronger than you tire more or less than yours? How about the muscles of people weaker than you?

BODY FACTS

It's easy to find a person's height, weight, and age, but the things that really count in terms of shedding excess heat or estimating body fat percentages are the body surface area, volume, and density.

Develop methods that enable you to determine the surface area, volume, and density of a person's body.

9
PLANT
SCIENCE

*W*hen you think of plants, you probably have visions of green trees and pretty flowers, but plants vary from tiny one-celled yeast or bacteria to giant redwoods. Green plants provide us with the food and oxygen we need for life. But it is the bacteria and fungi that decompose dead organic matter back into the chemicals essential for new life.

DECOMPOSITION RATES

Obtain a few handfuls of tree leaves. What can you do to increase the rate at which these leaves decompose? What can you do to decrease the natural decomposition rate of the leaves?

SEED DISPERSAL

Seeds are distributed in various ways. Sometimes it is the wind that spreads seeds. Have you ever noticed the *wings* on maple seeds? Sometimes seeds are spread by animals or water.

Collect seeds and/or fruit from as many plants as possible. See if you can determine how each plant disperses its seeds. What special mechanisms for dispersal can you find? Are some seeds dispersed in more than one way?

BLOOMING WILDFLOWERS

In the spring, summer, and fall, open fields are often filled with colorful wildflowers. If you look at these flowers carefully, you will see that as temperature, length of day, rainfall, and other conditions change so do the species of wildflowers that bloom.

Does the height of the flowers in bloom change with the season? Are the flowers that bloom in May as tall as those that blossom in September?

In a field or park in mid-May find as many blooming wildflowers as you can. Measure the height of the blossom above the ground of at least ten specimens of each species. Take an average of all your measurements to get a value for the average blossom height in May. If possible, collect, dry, and preserve a sample of each species. Repeat this experiment each month until autumn's cold brings blooming to an end.

A bar graph of your results may help you to see if the average height of flowers is related to the time of year. Does the average height of wildflowers change as the year progresses from spring to fall? If you find a pattern, can you offer an explanation?

SEPARATING
PLANT PIGMENTS

You know that leaves contain colored pigments. After all, most leaves are green, but in autumn other colors appear. To separate the pigments in leaves you can use a technique called paper chromatography.

CAUTION: This project involves chemicals. Work in a well-ventilated area and wear your safety goggles.

Collect a variety of leaves. Then, while the leaves are still fresh, cut strips of filter paper about ¾ inch × 4 inches (2 cm × 10 cm). To transfer the pigment to the paper strips, place a leaf on the paper about ¾ inch (2 cm) from one end. Roll the edge of a coin or washer over the leaf so as to crush the leaf tissue. Repeat the process several times using a fresh part of the leaf over the same place on the paper each time. Prepare one strip like this for each type of leaf you collected.

After the leaf tissue on the paper has dried, use tape to hang the strips, in groups of two or three, from a pencil or stick. The pigmented stripe should be farthest from the taped end of each paper strip. Lower each set of paper strips into a beaker that contains enough acetone (or fingernail polish remover, which is mostly acetone) to reach the bottom of the strips and a little higher so that the liquid can ascend the strips. However, the acetone should be below the strip of crushed leaf tissue. **Handle acetone with care. It is flammable and toxic. Try to avoid its vapors by covering the beakers.** The pencil will support the strips and allow you to watch the ascending acetone carry different pigments to various heights along the paper. You may want to change the length of the paper strips to get better separation of pigments.

Let the strips dry. Then look at the pigments that have been separated. Which leaf contained the most pigments? By placing each dry paper strip next to the leaf from which the colors came, you will have an interesting display.

Can alcohols such as grain, wood, and rubbing alcohol be used to separate pigments?

EXPERIMENTS WITH
SEEDS AND SEEDLINGS

Using bean or corn seeds; plastic, cardboard, or other containers; and vermiculite or soil for the seeds to grow in, you can investigate a number of factors that influence seed and seedling growth.

To begin, you might try to find out if seeds will germinate underwater, or whether seeds need any water at all to germinate. Do deeply planted seeds grow better than those planted close to the surface? Will seeds germinate in the dark? Will seedlings grow in darkness? If they do, how does their growth compare with that of seedlings grown in light? Can you predict what will happen if you cover the leaves of a seedling growing in light? Will seeds kept in a freezer germinate? Will seedlings left in a freezer overnight continue to grow? Over what temperature range can seedlings grow? Will seedlings grow in saltwater?

Can a seedling survive if you cut off its root? if you cut off its leaves? if you cut off what remains of the seed after it has germinated?

Place a growing plant near a window. Does it bend toward the light? If it does, what happens when you turn it around? Does its direction of growth change again? Does the color of light affect the direction of a plant's growth? Do plants grow better in light of a particular color? Suitable filters can be obtained from Rosco Laboratories, 36 Bush Avenue, Port Chester, NY 10573.

Plant some seeds in a clear plastic container so you can watch as they germinate. Which way do the roots grow? Which way do the stems grow? Once the seeds have germinated, turn the box on its side. What hap-

*This oat seedling
has an affinity
for blue light.*

pens to the direction of growth of the roots and stems
now? Can you use light to make stems grow down
instead of up?

Put a sheet of cardboard on an old phonograph
turntable. To the cardboard fasten a container of seedlings growing in vermiculite. Be sure the weight,
which should not be large, is evenly distributed along
the diameter of the turntable. Let the seedlings rotate
for several days. What happens? How do they compare with a control group?

Does the rate of rotation affect the direction of
growth? Does the distance of the seedlings from the
center of the turntable have an effect? What happens
to the growth pattern after the seedlings stop rotat-
ing?

If you have trouble understanding the results of
your rotating-plant experiments, read some books
that discuss ways of creating an artificial gravity in
space.

Let some seedlings grow in soil until they flower
and produce their own seeds. When the seeds are dry,
collect them. Plant some of the seeds right away. Store

others for several months before planting. Store some in a freezer, some in a refrigerator, some in a warm place, and the rest at room temperature—half in darkness and half in light. Do all the seeds germinate? What conditions seem to be the best for storing seeds? Is this true of all types of seeds?

CLONING PLANTS

Cloning means the reproduction of genetically identical organisms. This is difficult to do in higher animals, but some plants can be cloned by taking a cutting from an existing plant. One common method is called *rooting*.

To clone plants, first build a "bed" for rooting. To do this, punch some good size holes in the bottom of a plastic container (an old dishpan works well) with a large nail. The holes will allow excess moisture to drain away and prevent the plants from rotting. Put a piece of paper towel or facial tissue over each hole and pour in sand or vermiculite to a depth of about 6 inches (15 cm). Add water to moisten the rooting bed.

Start with a coleus plant, which is easy to root. Use a sharp knife to cut off a plant about 2 inches (5 cm) above the soil in which it is growing. Will the plant that has been cut off continue to grow generating new stem and leaves?

Trim off the lower leaves of the plant you have cut away and stick its stem into the rooting bed soil. Make several similar cuttings.

Use coat hanger wire and plastic sheeting to build a greenhouse that covers the bed like the one shown in Figure 30. Place the bed in an area that receives light but not direct sunlight. Lift the plastic and feel the soil every day. If it feels dry, add some rainwater or tap water that has been allowed to sit for several days so that the chlorine can escape.

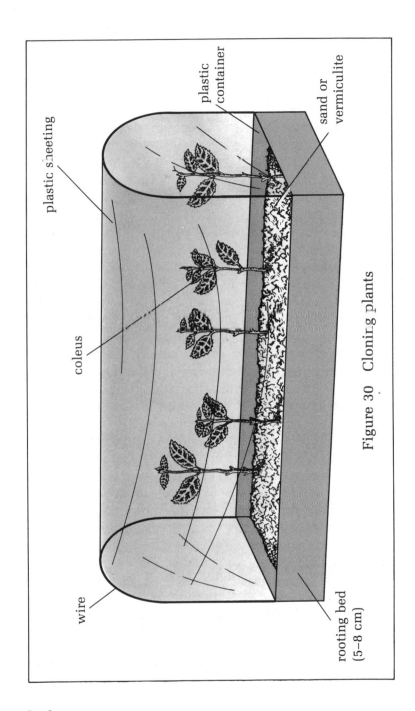

Figure 30 Cloning plants

plastic sheeting

plastic container

sand or vermiculite

coleus

wire

rooting bed (5–8 cm)

After two weeks, reach under the plastic and give the plant a gentle tug. If it moves easily, leave it for another week, but if it seems to be firmly implanted, dig around the plant and remove it. Has the plant grown new roots?

Try rooting other plants such as chrysanthemums, philodendrons, ivys, African violets, begonias, and geraniums, using this method. Will some of these plants root if you use a single leaf? Can you get a bean plant to root? Cut the stem of a bean plant about 3 inches (8 cm) below the cotyledon leaf remains and place it in the rooting bed. Will it take root? Will the old root and remaining stem regenerate a new plant?

Design an experiment to find out how temperature affects the rooting process.

There are substances that are supposed to speed up the rooting process in plants. Buy some at a flower or garden store and design experiments to see if the stuff really works. To see if other chemicals will induce rooting, trim some bean plants as shown in Figure 31. Place five or six in pint containers of water and other chemicals. Prepare a boric acid solution by adding a teaspoonful of the white powder to a gallon of water. Put a teaspoonful of the solution into one of the pint containers of water with bean cuttings. Observe the plants over several weeks. Try different concentrations of boric acid as well as salt, sugar, and baking soda and special rooting chemicals. How do these various chemicals affect the rooting?

NOT THE LEAST IS YEAST

As you may know, bread rises because cooks add yeast to the dough. Yeast is a single-celled plant, a type of fungus that cannot manufacture food because it lacks the chlorophyll characteristic of green plants. When yeast cells respire, they change certain foods

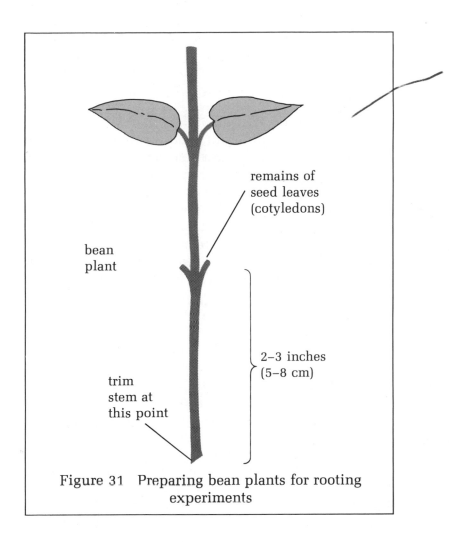

remains of
seed leaves
(cotyledons)

bean
plant

2–3 inches
(5–8 cm)

trim
stem at
this point

Figure 31   Preparing bean plants for rooting
experiments

into alcohol and carbon dioxide. Bubbles of carbon
dioxide trapped in the sticky dough causes bread to
rise.

You can do an experiment to find out which foods
yeast likes best. You won't be able to detect the alcohol, except by its odor, but the bubbles of carbon dioxide can be seen easily.

To make a yeast culture, add a tablespoonful of dry yeast to a cup of warm water. Stir until the yeast dissolves. Put a tablespoonful of the solution into each of a dozen or more medicine cups or the empty cups of a muffin tin. In one cup leave just the solution. It will serve as a control. To each of the other cups add about ¼ teaspoonful of different food samples. You could use flour, table sugar, brown sugar, powdered sugar, sugar substitutes, cornstarch, salt, milk, chopped meat, cooking oil, and pancake syrup. Keep a record and diagram so you will know which food is in each cup. Stir the cups with a clean straw or stirring rod. Which cups show immediate evidence of carbon dioxide? Be sure to rinse the rod or straw thoroughly after each stirring so that material is not transferred from one cup to another.

Put the cups in a warm place or in an oven heated to 150°F (66°C). After a few minutes check to see which cups contain foamy bubbles of carbon dioxide. Put the cups back for another 5 minutes and check again. Are any of the samples slow starters?

Which food type seemed to produce the most carbon dioxide? Which food samples seemed unaffected by the yeast when compared to the control?

Use the same or a similar solution to see if the concentration of sugar affects the production of carbon dioxide. Vary the concentration from ¼ to 2 teaspoonfuls in a tablespoonful of yeast solution. After warming, compare the samples with one another and the control.

Design an experiment to see how temperature affects the production of carbon dioxide by yeast.

For a more quantitative investigation of the effect of temperature on carbon dioxide formation by yeast, set up the apparatus shown in Figure 32. Nearly fill the test tube with a solution of yeast and sugar made from a tablespoonful of yeast and 3 teaspoonfuls of

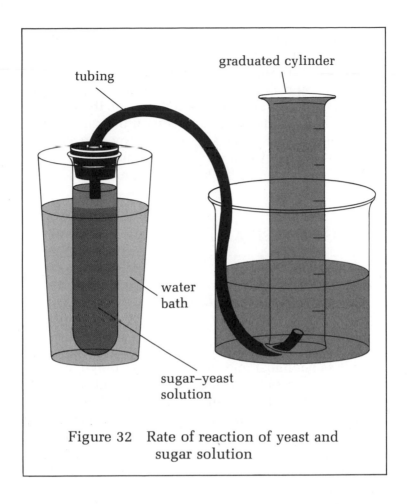

tubing

graduated cylinder

water
bath

sugar–yeast
solution

Figure 32   Rate of reaction of yeast and
sugar solution

sugar in a cup of warm water. Fill the water bath with
water at a particular temperature from 32°F (0°C) to
150°F (66°C). Maintain that temperature throughout
the run by adding hot or cold water or ice.

After the set up has been established for 5 minutes
to allow the temperature to become uniform throughout, fill the graduated cylinder with water, invert it,
and place it over the end of the tubing. Carbon dioxide
produced in the test tube will replace water in the

graduated cylinder. Record the time and the volume of gas produced every 30 seconds for 15 minutes. Repeat the experiment at various temperatures.

Plot a graph showing the volume of carbon dioxide produced on the vertical axis and time on the horizontal axis. Plot the data for each run on the same graph. This will give you a graph for each temperature on the same set of axes. What do your graphs reveal?

How might you improve the design of this experiment?

PHOTOSYNTHESIS AND LIGHT

> **REMINDER**
> Don't forget your safety goggles.

The world's green plants can "capture" light and store it as chemical energy in the food they manufacture. The process by which they manufacture food is called *photosynthesis*. During photosynthesis, green plants use the light from the sun to convert carbon dioxide and water into food and oxygen. The food contains more energy than the water and carbon dioxide from which it was made. The added energy came from sunlight.

The oxygen formed during photosynthesis is the gas we breathe. Since only green plants carry on this magnificent process, the earth's entire source of food and oxygen comes from green plants. Without them, life as we know it would be impossible.

But there are life forms, found on the sea-bottom, that thrive on sulfur-rich waters that emerge from vents in the ocean floor. Bacteria use the sulfur to manufacture food without the presence of oxygen.

To see that light is essential for food production in green plants, you can test some leaves that have been in light and compare them with leaves that have been in the dark before testing. The test consists of finding out whether there is starch (food) in the leaf tissue.

Prepare some Lugol's solution by dissolving 5 g of iodine and 10 g of potassium iodide crystals in 100 ml of water. Add a drop or two of the solution to a suspension of starch in water. The dark-blue color produced when iodine reacts with starch serves as a test for starch.

Completely cover one leaf on a geranium plant with black paper. Use paper clips to hold the paper in place. Cover another leaf with a piece of black paper that has a circular hole in it. Expose the plant to a bright light for 24 hours. Remove the two leaves that were covered or partially covered as well as one leaf that was exposed to light. Break the cell walls in these leaves by placing the leaves in boiling water.

Once the leaves are limp, you can extract the chlorophyll from the leaves by placing them in hot alcohol. **Warning: Do not heat alcohol with an open flame.** Put the alcohol in a small beaker, which can be placed in a larger beaker that contains water. Heat the water with an electric hot plate. You will see the leaves grow pale as their chlorophyll dissolves in alcohol. When the leaves are quite pale, remove them with forceps and put them one at a time into a shallow bath of Lugol's solution. Starch, which is not soluble in alcohol, will take on the characteristic dark-blue color if present.

What evidence do you have to indicate that light is essential for photosynthesis?

Design another experiment to show that carbon dioxide is required for photosynthesis. Design one to detect the release of oxygen during this process.

10

ANIMAL

SCIENCE

There are a great variety of animals on earth. You can't possibly investigate all of them, but these projects should allow you to study some of them.

SPYING ON BIRDS

With a field guide to help you, you can begin a study of the birds that live in your area. A pair of binoculars will provide an opportunity to view birds more closely, but they are not essential. In a notebook keep a list of all the birds you see, where you see them, when you see them, and what they are doing.

When you find a bird that you haven't identified, ask yourself these questions: How big is it compared to birds you already know? What shape does it have? Is it chunky or slender? Is its bill long or short? Is its head crested? How does it move? Does it fly in straight lines, weave up and down, dart to and fro, or soar? On the ground, does it walk or hop? Or is it a water bird that glides along the water surface? What are its markings? Its colors? Does it sing a characteristic song? What does it eat? What does it feed its young? What are its eggs like? Do both males and females care for the young?

Once you've learned to identify the birds where you live, study them in a more scientific way. How can nests be used to identify birds? How do birds build them? Where do they build them? What do they eat? Which migrating bird returns first in the spring? Do both sexes return together, or does one precede the other? Which species stay through the winter? Make a sample count of each species from time to time. Does the relative number of each species change from season to season or even from week to week?

Build or buy a bird feeder. Put it in a sheltered place where you can observe the birds that come to feed. Which birds are attracted to grains of wheat or corn? Which ones like fat trimmings or suet? Do any like peanut butter? jelly?

Using food coloring, color sunflower seeds with different colors. Do birds seem to be attracted to, or repelled by particular colors?

Do some birds chase other birds away? Do some birds carry the food away rather than feasting at the feeder? Which birds dart in for a quick bite and then leave? Which ones stay for a more leisurely dinner? Do some feed in groups while others dine alone?

BY A FIREFLY'S LIGHT

When oxygen combines with a chemical called lucif-erin, a cold light (bioluminescence) results. It is this reaction that produces the light of the firefly. Is the rate of this firefly reaction related to the temperature of the environment? To find out, catch a firefly and put it in a small bottle or vial. Plug the opening of the vial with cotton or a porous material so that gases may pass to and from the vial. Lower the temperature by surrounding the bottle with ice cubes. Does the fire-fly's flash rate change? What happens to the flash rate if the firefly is placed in a warm environment?

Make a number of trials of this experiment. Care-fully record both the flash rate and the temperature over a wide range of temperatures. Plot a graph of the results. Do you find any mathematical relationship between flash rate and temperature?

Design an experiment to see how the concentra-tion of oxygen affects the firefly's flash rate. Release the firefly when you are through experimenting.

THE CARE, FEEDING, AND
STUDY OF MEALWORMS

By watching mealworms (larvae of the darkling bee-tle) you can observe the life cycle of an insect and have an interesting animal to study.

Buy 100 to 200 larvae or pupae from a pet store or a biological supply house. Put them in a plastic, metal, or glass container that is at least 6 inches (15 cm) on a side. Cover the base of the container with a 2- to 3-inch (5- to 8-cm) layer of food—oatmeal, wheat bran, crushed dog biscuits, or chicken laying mash. The animals can get their water from fruits and vegetables such as carrots, potatoes, or apples placed, uncut, on top of the food. Keep the food dry so it does not mold. Replace the pulpy fruits or vegetables whenever they seem to be dried out. The container should be covered with a sheet of cardboard placed on top.

When the larvae form pupae, remove the pupae to another container with a small amount of food until the adult beetles emerge. The adults can then be returned to the original culture. If you leave a few pupae in the large container, you will see why it is advisable to remove them.

If you note the pungent odor of ammonia or see mold in the food, it is time to move the animals to fresh food in another container. Should the container become crowded with adults and larvae, move some of them to a new container.

How long does it take these animals to go through a complete life cycle?

Mealworms (larvae) make interesting subjects for investigating animal behavior. Here are some questions that may serve as a framework for a series of experiments:

Do mealworms prefer light or darkness? How do mealworms respond to touch? Does it matter where you touch them? How do they respond to heat? To the odor of ammonia? To vinegar? Can you make a mealworm back up? Can they learn? Can they see? Can they hear?

SOW BUGS

One of the few crustaceans to successfully carve out a niche on land is the sow bug, commonly called the pill bug or wood louse. You can find these isopods under

Sow bugs

stones and logs, where they feed on decaying vegeta-
tion. If you have trouble finding them, you may be
able to attract some by leaving hollowed-out raw potatoes in moist shaded areas.

You can culture sow bugs on a mixture of sand
and peat moss in a coffee can or plastic container.
Keep a moist sponge in their home and add a fresh
piece of raw potato or carrot from time to time. Watch
these animals for a few days and try to decide what
conditions of temperature, light, and moisture they
like best. After you have formulated your hypotheses,
run some experimental tests.

Cover the bottom of a deep container with sand.
Bury three petri dishes or large jar lids in the sand so
that the edges of their open tops are level with the
sand. In each dish or lid place some peat moss. Thoroughly soak the moss in one dish. Moisten the moss in
a second dish; leave the moss in a third dish completely dry. Cover half of each dish with a piece of black
construction paper so that the moss under the paper

will be in darkness. Put a bright light above the container. Then place about a dozen sow bugs in the center of the container. Watch carefully. Where does each of the bugs finally come to rest? Were your hypotheses about light and moisture correct?

Design an experiment to test your hypothesis about the temperature the bugs prefer.

INSECTS IN THE DARK

The night air often is a source of insect activity. You can attract and capture insects of the night with a light and a sheet. Insects will fly a "spiral" path around the light, and some of them will settle on a white sheet hung beside the light. How many settle on the sheet after 20 minutes? Examine these insects. What kind do you find? Repeat the experiment for a number of nights. Does the number of insects that collect vary from night to night?

To trap the insects, secure a paper plate near a light bulb. Then lay strips of sticky flypaper along the plate. What conditions seem to affect the nighttime insect population? Is it temperature? wind? humidity? clouds?

Does the kind of insect flying about at night change with the season? For example, do you find June bugs only in June? What do you find when you try this experiment on comparable nights with regard to weather, at different times of the spring, summer, and autumn?

Design an experiment to see whether the color of the light plays a role in attracting insects.

COLLECTING SPIDER WEBS

Have you ever watched a spider spin a web? You'll find it fascinating, and you can preserve the web.

Use a spray can of white paint to paint the web lightly on both sides. Hold the can at least 2 feet (about 60 cm) from the web so as not to damage it. Start at the web's center and move outward. While the web is still tacky, hold a heavy sheet of black construction paper gently against it. With a fine brush, carefully break the points where the web is attached to its points of support.

When the paint is dry, spray on several light coats of clear varnish or cover the sheet with plastic wrap to preserve the web and seal it to the paper.

You can collect and compare the webs made by different species of spiders. And you can watch one spider and collect the webs it makes. Do the webs change as the spider ages?

If you have the patience to be a spider watcher, you'll find it worth your time. How do spiders catch their food? How do they eat their prey? Do they gulp their food or do they enjoy a long dinner hour? How do spiders reproduce? If possible, place a sac of spider eggs in a jar and watch for them to hatch. Once they hatch, release them or they will eat each other. Watch several of them after they leave the jar. What do they do? Young spiders often disperse by a process called *ballooning*. What is ballooning? Try to observe it.

SWEEPING FOR INSECTS

Insects are very abundant in temperate and tropical climates. You can see this for yourself by *sweeping* for insects.

To make a sweeper, first find an insect net or make one from a cheesecloth bag, stiff wire, and an old broom handle. Then walk through an open field that has tall grass and weeds growing in it. As you walk, swing the net back and forth through the grass and weeds. After you've swept a swath across the field, grab the bag at the center and twist it several times to trap any insects you may have captured. Cover the net with a large plastic bag and tie the top of the bag to the handle of the net. Now untwist the net and turn it inside out to release the insects into the plastic bag.

How many insects did you catch? How many different species do you see? Can you identify them? What else do you find in the net?

Repeat this experiment at different times of the year. When are insects most abundant? Do you always catch the same kinds of insects, or do the species vary from month to month?

BREATHING FISH

You're right, fish don't breathe. But they do respire just like all living things. When a fish gulps water, it isn't swallowing the water. The water taken in passes over the blood-vessel-rich tissue that makes up its gills. The gills are located under those flaps of skin that lie behind a fish's eyes. A fish gulping water is the equivalent of a mammal breathing. Both are taking oxygen into, and expelling carbon dioxide from, their blood. However, a fish is cold-blooded; its body temperature changes with the temperature of its environment.

Do you think the gulping rate of a fish will change as the water temperature changes? Will a fish's activity level affect its gulping rate?

To find out, you'll need four goldfish, preferably Comet goldfish. Comets can withstand changes in water temperature quite well. You'll also need two tanks. Flat-sided tanks work best. They don't make the fish appear distorted the way round bowls do. Place two fish in each tank with water at 70°F (21°C). If you use chlorinated tap water, let it stand for several days before putting fish in it.

When the fish seem quiet and are used to your presence, count the gulping rate of each fish in gulps per minute. Make several counts and take an average. Then slowly raise the water temperature in one tank to 75°F (24°C) by adding and stirring in warm water. In order not to shock the fish, it should take at least 20 minutes to make this temperature change. Similarly, and again at a very slow rate, lower the temperature in the other tank to 65°F (18°C). After the temperatures in the two tanks are steady and the fish are quiet, record their gulping rates again.

Lower the temperature in the cooler tank, slowly as before, to 55°F (16°C). This should take at least 45 minutes. Raise the temperature in the other tank to 80°F (26°C). If the fish begin swimming to the surface as the water warms, stop adding warm water.

When these temperatures are achieved and the fish are quiet, again measure their gulping rates. What is the effect of temperature on the respiration rate in fish? How can you make goldfish more active? How does their activity level affect their gulping rate?

Does the size of the fish seem to affect its respiration rate? How about the brightness of light around the tank? Does sound affect their respiration rate? Is classical music soothing to fish? Can you find other factors that affect a fish's respiration rate?

How is the solubility of oxygen in water related to temperature? How is it related to your data? Why do fish in some lakes and streams often die during hot summer months?

See if you can find out why fish appear distorted in round tanks.

ANIMAL TRACKS

When animals walk in snow or soft dirt, they leave tracks. The tracks you most commonly see are those made by dogs or cats. Look carefully at tracks you know were made by a dog and a cat. How do the tracks compare? How many toes do these animals have? Does either animal leave toenail tracks? How do their walking patterns compare?

After a light snowfall, take a walk in the woods. Bring along a book that contains drawings or pictures of the footprints of common animals. How many different kinds of animals walked through the woods you visited?

You can preserve animal tracks in a variety of ways. One method is to photograph or draw pictures of the prints you see. It's a good idea to place your own print next to the animal's. In that way, you can compare the relative sizes of the prints. You can cut silhouettes of the tracks from construction paper and paste them on white paper.

To make casts of footprints made in dirt, mix plaster of paris with water. When it has the right consistency, pour it into the track until it flows over the sides. Wait 20 minutes for the plaster to harden, then cut around the cast with a dull knife and lift it from the ground. Wash off the dirt and you will have a permanent record of the track.

To make a cast of a footprint left in snow, the temperature should be below freezing. Sprinkle a little water into the track. The water will freeze to make a thin coat of ice over the track's surface. This will help prevent the weight of the plaster from misshaping the track. Mix some snow in with the plaster and water so that it is cold. Pour the plaster into the track very slowly so as to melt as little snow as possible.

Melted paraffin can also be used to make casts of tracks, but this is difficult unless you have some way to melt the wax. Of course, you could tip a burning candle and let the melted wax flow into the track, but this method will take a long time.

BIBLIOGRAPHY

Beller, Joel. *Experimenting with Plants*. Arco, 1985.

Clark, John G. and Stone, Harris. *Science Project Puzzlers*. Prentice-Hall, 1981.

Cobb, Vicki. *Science Experiments You Can Eat*. Harper and Row, 1972.

Gardner, Martin. *Entertaining Science Experiments with Everyday Objects*. Dover, 1981.

Gardner, Robert. *Kitchen Chemistry*. Messner, 1982.

Research Problems in Biology Investigations for Students. Oxford University Press, 1976.

Stone, George K. *Science Projects You Can Do*. Prentice-Hall, 1963.

Van Deman, Barry A., and Ed McDonald. *Nuts and Bolts: A Matter of Fact Guide to Science Fair Projects*. The Science Man Press, 1980.

Webster, David. *Track Watching*. Watts, 1972.

_____ *How To Do A Science Project*. Watts, 1974.

Wells, Robert. *Science-Hobby Book of Bird Watching*. Lerner, 1968.

Wood, Elizabeth A. *Science from Your Airplane Window*. Dover, 1975.

INDEX